GIMME SHELTER

GEM

GOTCHA

GETAWAY

A Trilogy of Plays by
Barrie Keeffe

GROVE PRESS, INC., NEW YORK

Gem and *Gotcha* may be performed as separate short plays or as integral parts of the *Gimme Shelter* trilogy.

First published in Methuen New Theatrescripts in 1977 by Eyre Methuen Ltd, 11 New Fetter Lane, London EC4P 4EE, England.

First Evergreen Edition 1979
First Printing 1979
ISBN: 0-394-17419-4
Grove Press ISBN: 0-8021-4262-1
Library of Congress Catalog Card Number: 79-52013

LIBRARY OF CONGRESS CATALOGING IN PUBLICATION DATA

Keeffe, Barrie, 1945-
  Gimme shelter.

  Reprint of the ed. published by Eyre Methuen,
London, in series: Methuen new theatrescripts.
    CONTENTS: Gem.—Gotcha.—Getaway.
    I. Title.
PR6061.E32G55   1979   822'.8'14   79-52013
ISBN 0-394-17419-4 pbk.

Manufactured in the United States of America

Distributed by Random House, Inc., New York

GROVE PRESS, INC., 196 West Houston Street, New York, N.Y. 10014

'Listen my child, do not despair
for in the vampire you have a
friend and in the mite that infects
the mange you shall find another
friend.'

Comte de Lautréamont
Les Chants de Maldoror

Gimme Shelter was first produced as a trilogy at the Soho Poly Theatre Club, London on 1 February 1977 with the following cast:

KEV	Phillip Joseph
GARY	Ian Sharp
JANET	Sharman MacDonald
BILL	Roger Leach
TON	Roger Leach
LYNNE	Sharman MacDonald
KID	Philip Davis
HEAD	Peter Hughes

Directed by Keith Washington
Designed by Mary Moore
Lighting by Nick Chelton

The production subsequently toured Britain with Theatre Network Ltd and played a season at the Royal Court Theatre, London; the company was unchanged.

Note

The music indicated in this script is that used in the original production. This may be changed — the more contemporary the music, the better.

GEM

A play in three scenes

The first part of GIMME SHELTER

GEM was first produced on 7 July 1975 at the Soho Poly Theatre Club, London, with the following cast:

KEV	Will Knightley
GARY	Adrian Shergold
JANET	Sharman MacDonald
BILL	Michael Brodie

Directed by Keith Washington
Designed by Jane Ripley

The setting throughout is the boundary of a cricket pitch.

Music:
Before and after Scene One: Suzi Quatro's *Wild One*
Before Scene Three: Showaddywaddy's *Three Steps to Heaven*
After Scene Three: Gary Glitter's *Alright with the Boys*

Scene One

Morning. During the scene the light becomes brighter.
August Bank Holiday Monday. A bare stage, green. Stage right,
part of a white cricket boundary screen. The audience is the
cricket pitch.
Blackout. We hear Suzi Quatro's Wild One. *Lights up to reveal*
KEV, *holding a transistor to his ear. He stares at the audience,*
switches off the radio.
Pause.

KEV. Oh for the summer sun and the lush green fields of
    England. The gentle click of leather against willow.
    Cucumber sandwiches for tea and swallows in the twilight.
    (*He shouts.*) Come on you bastards, this'll do.

> KEV *sets down a plastic carrier-bag, takes out a can of beer,*
> *opens it, sips. He bounces a plastic football on his foot.*

GARY (*off*). Here, shot, shot —

> KEV *passes the ball to* GARY *who races onstage and kicks*
> *the ball behind the screen.*

GARY. Goal, what a goal! When's the season start? Here I am,
    charged up and raring to go like a bloody racehorse in his
    box.

KEV. This'll do, won't it?

GARY. Yeah, fine fine. Can't get further away from the pavilion
    than this, eh. Oi, Jan — come on.

> *Enter* JANET *and* BILL. *She is holding one shoe.*

JANET. I thought we was supposed to be watching a cricket
    match — not going on a cross country run. Shoe full of stones
    and I've got stung already.

GARY. Half way round the boundary and you're knackered.

KEV. Good job she didn't get in the team.

GARY. Would have needed an oxygen tent after every over.

KEV. He means — kiss of life.

JANET. Where?

KEV. That is a very good question. Answers on a postcard only.

BILL. I was going to offer to be Bondy's runner. But he couldn't afford me fee.

BILL *laughs, but the others don't. They're setting down their bags, taking in the view etc.*

BILL. It's going to be a hot day.

JANET. I hope so. We'll go back as brown as berries.

BILL. Mist over the sea. It'll be very hot once that cloud goes. Temperature in the seventies.

KEV. Thank you Bert Foord. Right, we'll stay here then shall we, for now?

GARY. All right. Drop everything.

JANET. Do you mind?

KEV. Oh yeah, going to be one of them days is it? All innuendo and no bloody action.

He makes a grab at JANET, *who evades him.*

JANET. Mind, they can see us from the pavilion.

KEV. So what. Give them something a bit more spunky than cricket to watch.

JANET. Here, what's that flashing?

GARY. Binoculars or something, in'it?

KEV. Flash bastards. I bet they never took that much hardware when they climbed Everest. Binoculars, telescopes, cine cameras, sun brollies, car chairs, lilos, picnic hampers — think they're on an expedition to Timbuktu — not a poxy cricket match at Thorpe Bay.

JANET. But I wish we'd stayed over there with them for a bit. Just for the morning, you know.

KEV. What? With them shits?

JANET. We could have had a laugh.

KEV. We'll have a laugh here, won't we.

JANET. You know what I mean, Bill?

BILL. Be like work though. I mean, you can't be yourself with that lot. Specially with their wives and everything with them.

KEV. That's dead right. A day with that lot and I'll end up in a bleeding loony bin. Ears permanently half cocked ready to

laugh every time Bondy or Leigh Hunt or Jackson cracks one
of their pissy little jokes. Be worse than the bloody coach
down here. Ooooo hooooo hoooo. Very good, sir.

GARY. Don't know how you do it.

KEV. Quick as a flash. Instant repartee.

GARY. Lightning wit.

KEV. Can't keep up with it. I heard that joke when I was sucking
me mum's tits.

GARY. Bad enough in Holborn.

JANET. Never speak to us in Holborn.

KEV. That's another thing. See, they do know our bloody names.

GARY. Right. When we stopped for the cuppa, in the bog. Leigh
Hunt was pissing next to me. Says: 'How you settling down
in marine, Parker?' Overlooking for a moment that I've been
in motor for the past eighteen months, he got me name right.
In the office, pass in the corridor, looks at me like I've come
to fix a Durex machine in the bog. Bastard.

KEV. All bastards.

JANET. Yeah, but it's different today, in'it. Firm's do.

KEV. Firm's do ought to be in firm's time. Firm's pay. Not a
bloody Bank Holiday Monday. No charging for the coach
fare either. Assets exceed 267 million pounds. 'Sorry old
boy, gotta charge for the coach. Seventy five p, pay Miss
Phillpot.' Pill in the pot's making a packet out of this.

GARY. Last year, though.

KEV. You bet. I tell you, there'll be some bloody changes here
once Clive Jenkins starts poking his nose in. There'll be some
bloody changes all right.

GARY. Right.

KEV. Bondy, St John, Jackson, Leigh Hunt — all of them with
the don't-piss-in-the-Windsor-soup voices'll be demoted to
messenger boys. You wait.

GARY. Right.

KEV. No buggering about then with the full weight of Clive
Jenkins behind us. They'll be petrified to try anything. One
out-of-place remark from Bondy, mate, and everybody out.

The whole insurance world will tremble. They'll be grounding planes, stopping ships and the entire capitalist world will come to a standstill. Bondy'll be out on his arse. A vagabond, smoking dog ends and looking for scraps to eat in the dustbins.

JANET. Did you see his wife?

BILL. I thought she was his daughter or something.

JANET. No, his wife. I saw her at the Christmas dinner at the Savoy. She's nice.

BILL. Bloody gorgeous.

KEV. What's she see in a gin soaked old sod like him?

GARY. Thirty-five grand a year?

KEV. More. Few hundred shares, house in Cyprus he hires out in the summer. Hand in the till. Still don't know his arse from his elbow and don't give a fuck whether it shows or not.

JANET. That's what I sorta like about him.

KEV. Like about him?

JANET. Sort of suave, you know. Sort of oozes out of him. 'I'm a snob, a twit and a piss artist. And so what?' Kind of attractive — to some people.

KEV. You better not let Clive Jenkins hear you say that.

JANET. But he knows, don't he. He knows how they all lick his arse, and buy him drinks and — he's taking the piss out of them in a very subtle way.

KEV. There is nothing more disgustingly bourgeois than an excess of subtlety. They should be starting any minute. Know what the team is?

BILL. Bondy opens the batting —

GARY. So they'll have to bowl underarm.

BILL. Then those two blokes out of computers are in, then Winston —

KEV. Is he playing?

BILL. Fourth man. They say he's a good bowler, off spin —

KEV. I know he's a good bowler. He got the chance to sign for Kent. But I didn't think he'd be such a snide shit to play for the firm's team. Didn't no-one give him the score?

GARY. He laughed.

KEV. He what?

GARY. Just laughed.

KEV. The patronising nigger. He's only been here a year and he's already playing cricket for bloody Bondy. I'll have to have a word with him.

GARY. Won't make no difference. I told him it weren't the done thing. And —

KEV. And what?

GARY. He just laughed. Said it was stoopid.

KEV. He's let the side down. Very badly.

JANET. Shut up Kev. What would you do if you was asked to play? You'd —

KEV. I'd tell them to go piss up their kilts, mate.

JANET. Yeah?

BILL. Might be different if you *was* asked —

KEV. Listen Billy Boy. The reason they haven't asked me is because I've made it pretty bloody obvious what my answer would be. They hate rejection. It's a sort of allergy they're very sensitive to, due to all the pure inbreeding.

GARY. They asked me to play football for them. When Jackson heard I'd been on Orient's books at school, he tried to get me to play for them. And they play on Wednesdays. Day off every week in the season, it would have been. Trip to Gibraltar at Easter. Talk of going to South Africa, play the subsidiary there. Laid out the temptations before me they did. I told Jackson what to do with it.

KEV. Good for you.

BILL. What did you say?

GARY. Well, I didn't make it blatant, like.

BILL. So what did you tell him?

GARY. Played it a bit close to me chest. No need to go arousing unnecessary hostility, I thought.

BILL. I see.

GARY. So I told him I'd got a dodgy cartilege and couldn't play. That was my official reason for declining his invitation. But he knew. He bloody knew all right.

KEV. Do all that, all sticking together, and then Winston — just sails off into the cricket team. Betrayed us. Long streak of piss.

JANET. If I'm laying here like this, they can see up me legs can't they.

KEV. Depends how bored they are by the cricket, love.

JANET. Harrr-bloody-harr.

KEV *sits.*

KEV. Christ. This is bloody lovely isn't it.

GARY. I'm sweltering already.

KEV. Janet, I'm stone cold sober and I fancy you already.

JANET. Tar.

KEV. Go swimming in the nude later.

JANET. The beach is packed. Like sardines.

KEV. Start a new trend, won't we. One year I'm going to go to St Tropez. They sunbathe their tits and no-one takes a blind bit of notice. All so natural and healthy and lustful. I'll have to keep a telephone directory on me cock to hold it down.

BILL. They're stark naked now.

KEV. You what?

BILL. St Tropez. They're naked. No costumes. They have lookouts with bugles. When the police come they blow their bugles and everyone puts on their pants.

KEV. I don't believe it.

BILL. Seen it.

KEV. Gerraway.

BILL. I was there in June.

KEV. In St Trop? I thought you was doing your bloody degree exams?

BILL. Afterwards. Mate and me went to France for a couple of weeks.

KEV. Fuck me. Students pissing off to St Trop while we're slaving over a hot accounts book. Tell me you're having me on.

BILL. You sound like my old man.

KEV. I thought you was jobbing at our place to get a bit of money for a holiday.

BILL. That's right.

KEV. Sod me. Where you going this one? Peking? Miami? Rio de Janeiro? World cruise?

BILL. I'm easy.

KEV. That's nice to know. Glad you're not fussy. What a bloody liberty. Spend six weeks flicking paper clips at Pill in the Pot and touching up the canteen girls and then calmly tell us while we're stuck in Holborn for the winter you'll be off to bloody Mexico or somewhere exotic.

BILL *laughs, takes off his shirt.*

JANET. That's what I call a suntan.

KEV. That's what I call a bloody V-sign to the working man.

JANET. What you studying Kev?

BILL. Marine biology.

GARY. Interesting.

BILL. I find it, interesting.

GARY. What'll you do afterwards?

BILL. Fish farming — ocean farming. Looking for food under the sea.

KEV. Christ Almighty, that sounds more like a holiday than your bloody holidays do.

JANET. Is it well paid?

BILL. Better be.

GARY. Do you need a degree to get into it?

BILL. Yeah.

KEV. How about for holding your snorkel?

BILL *laughs, sunbathes.*

GARY. What do you think of the office then? I mean, every summer we have students in. Always wonder what they think of it.

BILL. All right.

JANET. You just bugger about all the time. The older ones hate you.

BILL *laughs.*

KEV. The age gap is coming down by the minute. You have bloody got it made, Billy Boy. Haven't been tempted to stay, have you? Make a career in insurance? 'Cause if you have, I'll do a swap with you.

JANET. Anyone fancy an ice cream?

GARY. Yeah, all right.

JANET. Here's ten p. — get me one when you go.

GARY. Bloody cheek. What about you Kev?

KEV. One of those runny ones with a lump of chocolate in the middle.

GARY. Bill?

BILL. I'm easy.

GARY. Won't be a tick. (*He goes.*)

KEV. Nice bloke Gary, in't he?

BILL. Seems it.

KEV. He is.

BILL. Happy bloke.

KEV. Bloody right. If he was a bit taller, he'd be earning his crust as a footballer. Orient would have signed him. If he'd been a bit taller. When the Orient didn't sign Gary, his old man never spoke to him for a month. Like it was bloody Gary's fault. Oh Christ! Only another forty years and it'll be like this all the time.

The three lie there: silence for a bit. KEV's *hand starts to climb* JANET's *thigh.*

JANET. I'm watching you, Kev.

KEV. But can you *feel* me, Janet.

JANET. They might be looking through their binoculars.

KEV. So bloody what. Christ, Janet: you are so bloody sexy. (*He rolls on top of her.*)

JANET. Piss off.

KEV. I'm telling you. Everything about you turns me on. Last week, when you was wearing that see-through blouse, I made the Birmingham office's quarter yearly profit different by a hundred grand every time I added it up. I had to go and have a cold shower. I was in a lather of lust for you. Janet, I'm going to get you bloody drunk today. Helplessly out of control.

JANET. Have you got a girlfriend, Bill?

BILL. Huh huh.

JANET. Oh. Get off Kev, you're bleeding crushing me.

KEV. Let's go down to the beach Janet.

JANET. I'm trying to sleep.

KEV. After dark. Alone. Just the crushing of the waves and us.

JANET. What, and get sand in it and all?

KEV. Now that is very revealing. It means —

JANET. Oh shut up.

Applause off. KEV *walks to the edge of the boundary.*

KEV. They're coming out. And they're going to have their photo taken. It'll be in the autumn magazine. Christ Bill — you better put your name down or you won't get a copy.

GARY *enters with the ice creams.*

GARY. Leigh Hunt's whites look a nice yellow.

JANET. I thought they were his long johns.

GARY. Steaming with Vic chest rub.

KEV. Twenty-two blokes out there — and do you know something Bill boy. Not one of them knows the first bloody thing about insurance.

JANET. What's all the fuss?

GARY. Tossing up to see who goes in first — eh, Christ. None of them have got a coin!

KEV. Assets exceed 267 million and — bloody hell.

JANET. Do you reckon this grass is a bit damp?

KEV. Eh?

JANET. Only if it's damp, I better not sit here. See, there's a long history of piles in my family.

KEV. I tell you something Janet — I bloody wish you hadn't told me that.

> JANET *sits on her bag.* KEV *sits beside her again.* BILL *sits to one side.* GARY *stands bouncing the football on one foot, dribbles etc.*

GARY (*John Arlott voice*). Essex Division won the toss. . . going in on a good wicket.

KEV. I hope they run up a bloody landslide. See all those blokes there Billy. Know something, son. Not one of them knows a premium from a bloody Irish Sweepstake ticket.

BILL. Yeah?

KEV. Yeah. When I first came here. . . couple of years ago. . . heard about this fuss. Great fuss going on. There was this bloke caught screwing a secretary on the boardroom table. Night porter found them.

BILL. Yeah?

KEV. What did they do? Summoned a bloody board meeting. Wheeling them in in their bloody bathchairs. . . Leigh Hunt said: 'The bloke who was screwing her must go. Instant dismissal.' 'No', said Harrison. 'He's the only chap in the entire firm who can understand the computer.' 'Very well then,' says Leigh Hunt. 'The secretary must go. Instant dismissal.' 'No,' says Mrs Davies. 'She's the only typist in the entire firm that can spell.' 'In that case', says Leigh Hunt, 'the table must go.'

> *He laughs and rolls over stroking* JANET's *thigh. She motionless. He moves his hand under her skirt.*

JANET. I'm watching you Kevin.

KEV. But are you feeling me, Janet?

JANET. They might be looking through their binoculars.

KEV. So bloody what. Loosen the cobwebs on their cocks.

JANET. Hark at lover-boy. Some of them old blokes might surprise you. I know. I get invited to all the departmental parties at Christmas.

KEV. I wonder why that might be? I got it — you make the best sandwiches!

JANET. Ha. Oooh, the thicker the carpets, the faster passion throbs through the pin-stripes.

KEV. And the faster out come the heart attack pills.

JANET. You'd be surprised.

KEV. Surprise me then.

JANET. No, better not. I'll embarrass Billy.

KEV. I bet nothing embarrasses Billy, eh. Bloody university. Jammed pack full of non-virgo-intactas with their kaftans and screwed up skirts, eh. Blue stockings and black suspender belts and chanting Shakespeare's sonnets and smoking pot and fucking little rattlesnakes, eh. That right?

BILL (*reading his book*). Yeah.

GARY. Those student waitresses at Warner Bros —

KEV. Majorca.

GARY. Under thirties club. Best of both worlds. All the entertainment of a holiday camp and Spanish sunshine, see.

KEV. Couple of waitresses there was students. Biggest whores on the Costa Brava. . . so I was given to understand.

JANET. Not from personal experience, like.

KEV. Saving meself for you.

JANET. Oh yeah. Mug.

GARY. And he broke his leg —

KEV. Shut your bloody face, Gary.

GARY. Sorry I —

JANET. Oh yeah, forgot about that.

 She laughs.

KEV. It wasn't bloody funny —

JANET. No.

GARY. It weren't.

They try not to laugh, but suddenly snort.

KEV. Crutches for weeks. And I had to come in. Doctor wouldn't give me a bloody certificate.

JANET. Tell Billy how it happened.

KEV. The memory is too painful.

GARY. He was so pissed —

KEV. All right, all right.

GARY. He was pissed out of his mind —

KEV. Bloody smell of Bacardi now makes me puke.

GARY. See Bill, we thought — midnight swim. All rushed down to the pool, stripping of as we went — right abandoned — right mad we was — and Kev runs and leaps in the pool, like —

KEV. Stupid Spanish bastards had let out the water.

Laughter.

It weren't funny. I could have killed meself. (*Pause. Snorts of laughter.*) There was some disease going round or something. They was on a hygiene kick. No-one told me.

GARY. Make you laugh — when his leg was plastered up. Every night we went into the disco. . . they put on the same record. . . must have heard it a thousand times.

KEV. Very humorous are the Spaniards.

JANET. Your theme tune . . .

GARY (*sings*). 'I can't get no-oh — satisfaction. . .'

JANET and GARY. 'I can't get no-oh — girly action and I tried, and I tried . . .'

KEV. All right, all right. Leave it out. Seventy odd quid that holiday cost. Seventy quid for a half hundred weight of plaster and a bloody itching leg. (*Pause.*) Apart from that, it weren't so bad. Ever been to Spain, Billy. Lovely country —

BILL. Matter of fact, I was there at Easter.

KEV. Fucking Ada. This Easter?

BILL. Right.

KEV. Jesus. I suppose you do a bit of work now and again for a break, like.

BILL. It was a working trip. Near Alicante, they're doing some very exciting experiments with sea mosses.

KEV. I don't think I've the stomach for that sort of excitement.

BILL. Ten years time, your stomach'll be full of it.

KEV. I'm sure.

JANET. If you don't mind me asking —

BILL. What?

JANET. How do you afford it?

BILL. The faculty paid — it was very much a working trip.

KEV. I'm very pleased to hear that in no way could it be described as pleasurable.

'Howzat?' and applause off.

GARY. One down, nine to go.

JANET. Winston's bowled him.

KEV. He would. Hey, I think Bondy's touching Winston up.

JANET. Are we winning?

GARY. Only one wicket gone — for five.

KEV. What do you mean *we*?

JANET. I —

KEV. *They're* doing . . . not bad.

BILL. I'm surprised they all take it so seriously.

KEV. Seriously is not the word for it. The IRA could blow up the Stock Exchange, the pound could sink till it drowned and the Queen could turn out to be Lord Lucan in disguise. It still wouldn't be as bad as losing to Essex Division.

JANET turns onto her stomach.

KEV. Ooo, Christ Janet. Your arse don't arf turn me on. Pity it isn't where your face is, so we could admire it while you're sitting down.

JANET. You're mad.

KEV. Honest, I'm in a lather of lust for you. I'm going to get you bloody drunk today. Helplessly out of control and then. . . I shall impale you on me penis. (*He dives onto her.*)

JANET. Get off Kev, you're crushing me.

KEV. We'll go down to the beach, Jan.

JANET. I'm trying to get a suntan.

KEV. After dark, alone. While they're all whooping it up at the pavilion dance. We'll copulate with the salt air about our naked bodies, just the sound of lapping waves and faintly in the distance the three-piece band playing the Gay Gordons.

JANET. Oh piss off. You're embarrassing Billy.

GARY. And it's Ansell to bowl. Ansell, renowned throughout Sidcup for his roses, is about to try and prune Essex Division's batting. Harrr. Stopped at square leg by Winston —

KEV. Bloody Winston. I thought at least he might have had the decency to sabotage the game.

JANET. Do you like cricket, Bill?

BILL. Aye?

JANET. Cricket — do you like it?

BILL. Not bothered.

JANET. I think you're the first student to come to the match. Usually, the students in the summer don't come.

BILL. Experience. The brolly and bowler brigade at play. The pin-stripe brigade letting their hair down. Experience of a lifetime.

JANET. It's tonight they let their hair down. At the pavilion dance. Wait till you see them then —

BILL. Yeah?

JANET. You'd be amazed how they bugger about then. . . really show themselves up . . . Bondy and Leigh Hunt and . . . then tomorrow, at work, just like after the Christmas parties . . . can't meet your eyes . . . right laugh it'll be.

KEV. Pity we ain't going.

JANET. You what?

KEV. No use telling Billy all about it, seeing like that none of us are going to it.

JANET. The dance —

KEV. No.

JANET. You're kidding.

KEV. I'm not. We've got an agreement, love. Them. The shits — we said we'd not have anything to do with them all day.

JANET. But the dance in the pavilion tonight —

KEV. Or that.

JANET. Like hell.

KEV. Nothing to do with them Jan.

JANET. What was the bloody point of coming then?

KEV. Undermine them. Ruin their bloody day for them.

JANET. You're mad.

KEV. All of them over there — all four coach loads . . . they're all looking at us over here and they're saying to themselves: 'What the fuck are they doing over there?'

JANET. What *are* we doing over here?

KEV. We agreed. Getting under their skin. Bloody protesting — having nothing to do with them. Making them bloody uncomfortable.

JANET. And tonight —

KEV. Loads of things we can do. The pier — fairground up the road at Southend. We'll have a great time.

JANET. I'm not buggering off to Southend. I'm going to the bloody dance.

KEVIN *grips her arm.*

KEV. Jan —

JANET. You're hurting my arm.

KEV. Jan, it's them and us. Got to stick together.

JANET. Let go of my arm.

Pause. He releases her arm. She picks up her bag.

KEV. What you doing?

JANET. Fed up with this . . . bloody stupid. Going with the others.

KEV. But Jan — we're going to have a great day. We've got the beer, we've got the —

JANET. Bye (*She goes.*)

KEV (*shouts*). When Clive Jenkins gets in here — you'll be out on your arse.

JANET (*off*). Bollocks.

KEV. Charming in'it.

GARY. She's going.

KEV. Bloody bints. No sense of solidarity, eh.

GARY. No . . .

KEV. Wanted her mirror — flash it in bloody Bondy's eyes when he's batting.

GARY. Still buy one . . . somewhere.

KEV. Makes you sick, don't it, Bill. (*Pause.*) More beer for us. (*He opens a can.*)

   '*Howzat?' and applause off.*

GARY. Second wicket. Two for eleven.

KEV (*quiet*). If they're not careful . . . we're going to bloody win . . .

   Fade.

Scene Two

Lunch break in the match. KEV and GARY alone. GARY plays the guitar well and sings two verses of a slow Beatles' ballad.

KEV. You know something Gary, mate. You ain't got a bad voice.

GARY. Like a blocked up drain —

KEV. Nar —

GARY. Think it's the radiators playing up when I sing in the office —

KEV. Yeah well — singing there, what do you expect. Here, give us — (*He takes the guitar.*)

GARY. Play it?

KEV. At one time — a bit. What's G?

GARY. That there — no there then —

KEV. Never could get me bloody finger there while that one's there. More a pianist's hands, mine.

GARY. Too fat —

KEV. Know what I mean. Not guitar. Too sensitive for the guitar.

GARY. Oh.

KEV. Like falling off a log, musical instruments to some people. Take to them — easy. Aptitude. Still. (*He puts down the guitar.*) Can't be good at everything.

GARY. Right.

KEV. Sort of picked it up, did you?

GARY. Yeah.

KEV. Not learn from books — you can't learn from books. That's how I tried, see. Hopeless.

GARY. Started off from a book —

KEV. But you had a mate who really taught you?

GARY. Oh yeah.

KEV. That's the difference. Great thing to be able to play an instrument. A social accomplishment. Always welcome at parties and that if you can play the old johanna.

GARY. I'll say. Bloke who taught me the guitar — should have seen him on the piano. Christ. No training or nothing. Instinct. Ear. Free drinks in the boozers that had pianos.

KEV. You ought to do something with your singing and that. Guitar. Semi-pro — weekend nights in a pub. Packet there.

GARY. Ain't that good.

KEV. No-one's much good. Except the really good ones. You're bloody good.

GARY. Bloke who taught me. Reckoned I was all right. He got up this little band, gigging. Pubs and that. I tried once. By the Elephant — right rough house. Lots of Teds. All they wanted was Sha Na Na and Rockets stuff. First night, bloody fight. Beer bottles chucking — mirror smashed. My mate, the bloke who taught me the guitar, like — just kept playing. I thought, fuck me — there's cool. Know what, he was high. Stoned out of his mind. Like the music, lived for it. Part of gigging, then. I never fancied that.

KEV. Right. You did the right thing. Keep away from that stuff.
That's why I never bothered with my band —

GARY. I didn't know you had a band —

KEV. Oh yeah — couple of years ago.

GARY. I thought you couldn't play —

KEV. Drums.

GARY. Arr.

KEV. And sang a bit, you know. But . . . drug scene. Didn't want
all that. I quit, got out before they got me. If you're not into
drugs, no good. Bit of an outsider, bit of a loner. I didn't want
to get involved. Good band though. Good musicians. One of
them plays with Elton John's band. American tours, country
house and all that. Good mate. But — the price he's paid for
it all. He won't see forty.

GARY. Which one's that?

Pause.

KEV. Forget his name. (*Pause.*) I'm like that. End of chapter.
Forget it all. No good keep looking back.

GARY. Right.

KEV. Not like that now, though. I got in at the wrong time. You
ought to give it a try.

GARY. Never fancied it. You know, sort of felt all fingers and
thumbs, lost me voice — in company. Tell you the best times,
when I really liked it . . . With the Orient youth team . . .
great blokes. Like you feel you're all on the way . . . This one
season . . . great team — eight made it, one's had Under 23
cap . . . this season we had a great run in the Youth Cup . . .
you start travelling a bit when you get past the fourth round.
Until then, all the matches around London . . . we went up to
Birmingham . . . played at St Andrews — huge — night match,
under the floodlights . . .coming back, just the team and
manager and coach in the team bus . . .won 3-1 . . . great
feeling . . . like you're bigger than everyone else — couldn't
sleep that night . . . feeling so close — like they're all your
brothers . . . stopped at a Chinese on the way out of Brum . . .
manager bought us all great bag of take-away . . . cans of
lager . . . coming back stuffing ourselves . . . talking . . . like
in the early hours of the next morning, like how you talk

— real deep . . . got out me guitar . . . see, I'd taken it on the
first match, and it had become our lucky mascot . . . used
to sit in the back of the coach on the Motorway . . . all have
this singsong . . . and I'd play me guitar . . . they was great
nights . . .

Long pause.

Best times . . . guitar . . . them nights . . .

KEV. You shouldn't have given up the game, Gary.

GARY. They said I didn't have it . . . me size.

KEV. Fucking stupid reason. Napoleon's too short to join the
bloody Territorials . . .

GARY. I knew they was right. When they told me, one Tuesday
night, end of the season, April 18th. I knew they was dishing
out the Apprentice Pros . . . touch and go . . . and when they
told me . . . I went bloody berserk . . . I went . . . Christ . . .
but I knew they was right . . .

Pause.

KEV. Still . . .

GARY. Yeah.

KEV *takes a sandwich, eats, drinks his beer.*

They're taking their time.

KEV. Bloody champagne they have — lunch break, champagne
for the team. And their wives. Bloody vile drink. Ulcers, gives
you ulcers.

GARY. We had champagne when we got to the semi-finals. In the
changing room, they brought in a couple of bottles.

KEV. Lucky you didn't get to the final, mate. Stomach ruined.

GARY. Yeah.

KEV. 165 all out. If they had you and me playing — your off
spins and my fast bowling — we'd have scuttled them for a
handful of runs.

GARY. I know.

KEV. And *they* know. Bastards.

BILL *arrives from the beach. Jeans rolled up to his knees,
shoes in hand.*

BILL. Beach's like the Northern Line. Rush hour.

KEV. Help yourself to a beer, Billy.

BILL. Tar. Not out yet?

KEV. Only need an hour to scuttle this mob. I've seen some bloody bad teams but I reckon my granny and a couple of her mates could have knocked up a better total than them.

BILL. No answer to Winston's bowling.

KEV. Winston's finished. As far as I'm concerned. Winston has had it. He's had his last pint off me. I've got nothing against Blacks. I love my Black mates like me own brothers. But an educated Black is something else. No sense of solidarity with his underprivileged white brothers.

  BILL *laughs.* KEV *stares hard at him.*

BILL. No Janet then?

KEV. Better not show her face here again today.

BILL. Nor Winston?

KEV. Right.

BILL. You go on like this and —

  Pause.

KEV. And what?

BILL. Up to you.

KEV. Right it is.

  BILL *gently takes a handkerchief from his pocket, unwraps a shell and inspects it.*

KEV. What is it?

BILL. Bunodactis Verrucosa.

GARY. You what?

BILL. Wartlet. Gem anemone.

GARY. Let's have a look.

BILL. Careful — don't touch.

GARY. Beautiful . . . really beautiful. Inch long . . .

BILL. Just a mass of jelly but . . . see, in the water — (*He puts it in a cup.*) — expanding, like petals . . .

GARY. Jesus.

BILL. But not a plant . . . carnivorous animal. And they're not petals, but tentacles. About fifty . . . like harpoons . . . any small animal touches them, transfixed and injected with poison and . . . dead. Feel . . . no, won't harm you . . . feels sticky . . . right?

GARY. So small . . . See it Kev?

KEV. Yeah, I've seen them . . .

GARY. Only usually get them in Cornwall or perhaps the south coast . . . strange how it got here. Right out of place.

KEV. Tell you something — like to drop that down Janet's knickers —

He goes to take it. BILL *puts it back in his handkerchief.*

BILL. No. Without water, it'd die.

KEV. Janet'll be wetting her drawers later on —

BILL. No Kev — leave it.

KEV. For fuck's sake. It's only a bleeding anemone.

BILL. A special one. Here.

They stare at each other. KEV *shrugs.*

KEV. And that's what you spend all your time doing is it? Buggering about with them?

BILL. You've sussed me. (*He laughs.*)

KEV. Better than working for a living.

GARY. Not arf.

KEV glares at GARY.

Sort of. (*Pause.*) Do you know what I fancy? (*Pause.*) 'I fancy an ice cream.' An ice cream it is. 'Ask the others.' Fancy an ice cream?

KEV. Yeah, all right.

GARY. Bill —

BILL. They'll be melted time you get them back —

GARY. There's a van by the pavilion —

BILL. Okay. Tar.

GARY. Won't be a tick. (*He goes.*)

    Pause.

BILL (*strums the guitar*). Neat. Yours?

KEV. Gary's.

BILL. Play it?

KEV. He does.

BILL. Man of many talents.

KEV. How do you mean?

BILL. Footballer — plays guitar. Nice bloke.

KEV. He is. Bloody nice bloke. (*He lies back, face to the sun.*) Bloody good mate is Gary. We've had some times, I can tell you.

    Pause. BILL *strums five chords, puts down the guitar.*

BILL. The birds all like him.

KEV. Who?

BILL. Gary.

KEV. Yeah.

BILL. Talk about him, they do. Hear them as you go by the bog. Aren't they filthy, what they say?

KEV. I dunno.

BILL. You should listen. An education.

KEV. Right up your street then.

BILL. Oh yes.

KEV. I bet you don't arf take the piss out of us.

BILL. Why?

KEV. I would. If I was you.

BILL. Oh.

KEV (*gets up, restless*). Cousin of mine. Fords. Dagenham. Hundred quid a fucking week.

    BILL *whistles.*

KEV. Bet you won't get a hundred quid a week.

BILL. Doubt it.

KEV. Paid for the boredom. Suppose . . . maybe one day . . .

BILL. Fords? Eighty quid a week?

KEV. I dunno.

Pause.

BILL. Wait till Clive Jenkins gets in.

KEV *grunts.*

Be all right then.

KEV. Can you see that lot of . . . shadows . . . letting Clive
Jenkins in? Bill . . . they'd rather be machine-gunned by Mick
McGahey than have a union card in their pocket. Of their
Burton off-the-peg.

Pause.

Day after August Bank Holiday Monday . . . wearing grammar
school blazer . . . school badge lovingly having been removed
by mother . . . leaving slightly discoloured shape on the breast
pocket, pressed trousers, shiny shoes . . . Arsenal Supporters'
club tie, resembling at ten yards, perhaps a not bad tie . . .
reported at reception . . . wearily shown to lift by contemp-
tuous doorman . . . and up to the fourth floor . . . where
delivered to Mr Charles: quartermaster and commander-in-
chief of army, 400 strong, male . . .clerks . . . a great sea of
shiny arsed, elbow gleaming, blue serge wearing . . . male
clerks . . . hunched over desks . . . not permitted to smoke . . .
clocked in and out by Mr Charles' severe frown instead of
blue collar machine . . . some with chairs with arms won by
long service and . . . some with two square feet carpets,
functional decoration for . . . something . . . shown to desk
and . . . career launched.

Pause.

Do you have the *News of the World?* Me mum said one
Sunday, 'Here, do you know him?' And I read the story . . .
I'd been off a week with the flu . . . and what I'd missed!
Bloke, forty, grey face, smile sometimes . . . neat, courteous,
ordinary . . . house in Clapham . . . one Christmas he had a
Led Zeppelin album for his son . . . couldn't picture what his
son looked like . . . and there, his picture in the *News of the
World.* Man gone berserk one Sunday afternoon . . . smashed
to pulp the head of his wife and daughter and then gassed
himself . . . the son discovered it all Monday morning. Such a

normal man, such a nice ordinary decent . . . male clerk . . .
occupational hazard . . .

Pause.

(*His finger in the cup.*) It's changing colour . . .

BILL. They adapt to their surroundings . . . for protection
sometimes . . . sometimes, so they can pounce . . . on
unsuspecting creatures.

KEV. Which one is this?

BILL. Disguises itself . . . hidden in the mosses — so it can pounce.
Kill. Survive.

KEV. Gary's taking his time with those bloody ice creams.

BILL. What I can't understand is . . . you staying.

KEV. Me old man's brother wore a bowler hat . . . went to the
City . . . had a car. Only bloke we knew who had a car . . .
respected man . . . clerk in the city. Me old man, factory —
set his heart on me being like me uncle . . . grammar school
. . . enough O levels for clerking but nothing else . . . arrive to
discover . . . no money, no status . . . a brothel of seething
frustrations and bitterness . . . window cleaners laughing
through the windows at us . . . cunts . . . And yet . . .
sufficient education to be . . . outcast from . . . what me mates
do . . . educated to be disillusioned? I'm pissed.

Pause. Applause off.

BILL. They're coming out.

KEV. Bondy to open . . . they'll bowl underarm . . .

BILL. Mirror in his eyes?

KEV. Bondy . . . is like Janet says . . . real money . . . style . . . I
preserve my hatred for the pissy little clerks who ape Bondy
. . . serviette holders and Woolworth's plastic wine-racks and
. . . moderation and . . . palates and no bloody appetite . . .
mirror in their eyes . . . need a lot of mirrors.

They look at the game.

You watch Bondy, he even bloody bats with a bit of style.
Gear all gone yellow — but can see he could play at one time.
He'll go for ones so that Winston can do most of the running
. . . leg off the back foot — old man's stroke . . . good work.

BILL. Know your cricket?

KEV. Came here — thought sport — could give me a hitch . . . up . . . (*He lights a cigarette.*) Not in their bloody league. . . (*He holds his head.*)

BILL. You all right?

KEV. Too much sun gives me a headache . . . forgot me sunglasses . . .

Enter GARY, *he wears cricket whites. Long pause.*

GARY. They . . . was short . . . Leigh Hunt's . . . bit knackered . . . they . . .

KEV. What?

GARY. Talked me into it . . . somehow . . . I wasn't thinking . . .

KEV. Sure . . .

GARY. Straight up Kev . . . Seventh man . . . I'll screw them up . . . make out I'm putting on a show . . . won't go for runs . . . show what I could do . . . off the back foot, drives through the gulley . . . but . . . shan't go for runs . . . seventh column and all that.

Pause.

I better get padded up . . . Got your ice creams . . . (*He goes, giving the ice creams to* BILL.)

KEV *hesitates, then tips the anemone from the cup and stamps on it. He breathes deeply.* BILL *crouches beside it.*

BILL. You can't kill them . . . smash them . . . and they just grow . . . again . . .

Applause off.

Winston . . .

KEV. Six.

Blackout.

Scene Three

Evening. Twilight. Showaddywaddy song, off. Empty stage. Then we hear giggles and mutterings from behind the cricket screen. Then JANET *appears — pulling up her knickers and tugging down her skirt.*

JANET. Oh, I do feel better for that. It's like when you're trying
to sneeze . . . and someone keeps distracting you . . . makes the
eventual sneeze all the better.

GARY *appears, zipping up his jeans.*

GARY. Bloody sneeze!

JANET. You know what I mean.

GARY. Charming. You need a feather not a —

They laugh.

JANET. Could arf do with a drink.

GARY. You're pissed enough already —

JANET. No, something exotic. Not gin. Fed up with gin.
Something like sangria. Know it?

GARY. Won the 2.30 at Sandown —

JANET. Sangria . . . that's what I call a drink . . . brandy and
that orange spirit, whatever it is . . . and wine. You get it in
tall glasses with tons of ice and bits of cucumber and
tomatoes —

GARY. Tomatoes!

JANET. Or celery or something floating in it. Oh, it's exotic. We
drank that all the time in Lloret. Me and Pauline.

GARY. Old Pauline eh —

JANET. We're going again next month.

GARY. You and Pauline.

JANET. No, I'm going with Pia, cause Pauline's getting married,
she says, but I dunno . . . You been to Lloret?

GARY. No —

JANET (*tuts*). You ought to go. You haven't been nowhere if
you haven't been to Lloret. It's so lovely. Just like a little
fishing village . . . with discos, and you can get chips if you
ask special . . . and the hotel we go, they have this wine on the
table for every meal, as much as you like, and it's all included
. . . and nowhere closes till four in the morning and they're
arf smart, the boys . . . so lovely the way they treat you . . .
and it's all right 'cause they hate the Germans . . . but they've
arf got money, and they think nothing of taking you to this
open-air disco in the mountains *and* buying you a lovely

dinner *and* afterwards . . . (*As if she's just thought of it.*) I wouldn't mind living in Lloret. Last year when I got home I cried for two days . . .

GARY. Oh yeah?

JANET. I couldn't wait to get the photos. There was one left over so I got me mum and dad outside the flats and when they come back from Boots me mum said, 'Oooo, what a lovely hotel.' And I said, 'You are daft, that's our bloody flats.'

GARY. Har.

JANET. He phoned me every Tuesday and Saturday night.

GARY. Who did?

JANET. Javeier.

GARY. Did he.

JANET. He said he was saving up for the ticket . . . to come to East Ham . . . but he never did . . .

GARY. You've got dirt all over your cardigan at the back.

JANET. Brush it off then . . . nice of Bondy . . . bottle of champagne.

GARY. Good innings I had —

JANET (*smoothing her skirt*). You can say that again.

GARY. Christ. Kev'll go spare.

JANET. Sod Kev.

GARY. I think he fancies you —

JANET. I don't want you to think I usually do this.

GARY. No —

JANET. Well . . . I think it's the sun . . . after a day in the sun at Lloret. . . oh, it's a different world. You ought to go to Lloret, Gary, really you did.

GARY. I'll come with you and Pia.

JANET. It's all so different out there —

GARY. Different out there. (*He looks at the cricket pitch.*) Didn't mean to but . . . when you're out there . . . and they're coming at you . . . you have to smash them . . . show who's governor . . . score off them . . . put them away . . . smash them . . .

JANET *puts on her shoes, does her lipstick etc.*

JANET. Got a comb?

GARY *gives her a comb.*

GARY. Kev should understand that. Easy to say you'll screw them up but —

JANET. I think I've really caught it today . . . me skin feels all stretched and . . . tingling with the sun. Just the smell of Ambre Solaire reminds me of Lloret.

GARY. I wonder where Kev and Billy are? Do you reckon maybe they went to the dance?

JANET. How should I know?

GARY. He said the Kursaal?

JANET. We'd better get back. I've got my reputation to think of —

GARY. According to form —

JANET. I don't want you telling no-one.

GARY. Course not.

JANET. I mean that.

GARY. I know.

JANET. Free agent.

GARY. Right.

JANET. Only young once.

GARY. Course you are.

JANET. Some people enjoy . . . knitting. No-one calls them an old bag because they enjoy knitting.

GARY. You what?

JANET. Miss Phillpot . . . I've heard her . . . going on. Know what she needs . . . ought to go to Lloret, be a different woman . . . not that one of the boys in Lloret would be interested in her. Old cow. She liked knitting, I don't look down me nose at her because she does knitting.

GARY. What the bleeding hell you talking about. First it's sneezing and now it's knitting. I've heard of euphemisms, but —

JANET. Do you mind!

GARY. Sorry I spoke.

JANET. Come on then. Might just have the Paul Jones with Bondy. The sun's brought his freckles out. He does look nice with his freckles showing.

GARY. Oh yeah?

They are beginning to go as KEV *enters from the other side, more drunk.*

KEV. Halt. Who goes there.

GARY. Kev —

KEV. The conquering hero. Fifty-six not out. Great innings.

GARY. Yeah?

KEV. Through the slips. Three times — six. Great shots. They never covered that.

GARY. Yeah —

KEV. Off the back foot, and all.

GARY. Pitching it —

KEV. Even the googlies — smash, smash, smash.

GARY. You saw —

KEV. I fucking saw all right. (*He grabs* GARY, *pushes him to his knees.*) What's your game —

GARY. Kev —

KEV. Whose side you on?

GARY. Kev, I didn't mean —

KEV. You didn't mean? Fan-tastic. Fucking fantastic. Fifty-six not out and he weren't trying! This boy will play for England. Janet — this is the greatest kiddo here.

JANET. Why don't you crawl in a hole.

KEV. I can't find one big enough.

JANET. Come on Gary, the tide must be on the turn. There's a funny smell.

KEV. When she talks I see it all in spelling mistakes.

JANET. It's only a game. There's no war going on —

KEV. That's just where you're wrong.

JANET. Am I? What part you playing then? Waiter in the NAAFI?

KEV. Piss off, slag.

JANET. You know what you need Kev? You need a therapeutic fuck.

KEV. Blimey. Where do you get that from? I must start reading *Angelique*.

GARY. Let go Kev . . . please . . . let —

JANET. You want to watch it Gary . . . I think he might be queer for you.

Pause. KEV *releases* GARY.

GARY. Listen Kev, really I mean —

KEV. Yeah . . . only kidding . . . great . . . I mean, it was good tactics. You showed them . . . I mean, out for a duck . . . that would have been too obvious.

GARY. Right.

KEV. Showed them what we could do —

GARY. Yeah . . .

KEV. If we chose to join them.

Pause. Enter BILL.

Thought you'd drowned.

BILL. Putting back the wartlet . . . needed rocks.

KEV. Coming for a drink then?

BILL. The pavilion?

KEV. Yeah, right Gary?

GARY. Well . . . sure.

KEV. Assets exceed . . . sink some of the profits.

BILL. Free bar?

KEV. Course not.

They go.

Fade. Music: Gary Glitter's Alright with the Boys.

End of play.

GOTCHA

A play in three scenes

The second part of GIMME SHELTER

GOTCHA was first produced on 17 May 1976 at the Soho Poly
Theatre Club, London, with the following cast:

TON	Derek Seaton
LYNNE	Polly Hemingway
KID	Philip Davis
HEAD	Peter Hughes

Directed by Keith Washington
Designed by Jane Ripley

The setting throughout is the small stockroom in the science
department of a large city comprehensive school.

Music:
Before the play: Rolling Stones' *Satisfaction* and *Street Fighting
Man.*
Before Scene One: Thunderclap Newman's *Something in the Air.*
Before Scene Two: Rolling Stones' *Get Off Of My Cloud.*
Before Scene Three: the Beatles' *Here Comes The Sun.*
Throughout Scene Three: the slow side of Rod Stewart's *Atlantic
Crossing* album.
After Scene Three curtain: Rolling Stones' *19th Nervous
Breakdown.*

Scene One

Thunderclap Newman's Something in the Air. *Music fades as lights rise on stockroom.*
A spring morning. The blind at the window is lowered.
A motor-bike dominates the room. TON *enters, a large man wearing a blazer over his football kit. He is smoking. He checks his watch, looks at the bike. He shuts the door, then sits on the bike, making an accelerating noise with his mouth.*
Enter LYNNE, *attractive, about 25. She carries books and papers. She puts them down, smiles.*

LYNNE. America should invade China and drop the atom bomb on Peking. (*She laughs.*) Fourth year . . . their unanimous verdict. McCarthy rules, OK?

TON *gets off the bike with difficulty.*

Hardly ton-up boy outfit.

TON. The match. Ten minutes, be starting.

LYNNE. Someone said, 'It'll take a stud nicely.'

TON. The pitch, the rain last night.

LYNNE. Connotation, word association. A stud. Thought they were talking about you.

TON. Lynne. This isn't easy.

LYNNE. Getting off the bike?

TON. Last day of term, shan't see you for a few weeks . . .

LYNNE. Is that all you wanted to tell me?

TON (*coughs, stubs out his cigarette*). I'm nay much of a talker . . .

LYNNE. Ideal qualification for a schoolteacher. Quintessential prerequisite for a career in education. I'm nay much of a talker . . .

TON. Lynne —

LYNNE. It's not yours, is it?

TON. Of course it isn't.

LYNNE. What's it doing here?

TON. No idea.

LYNNE. Perhaps it belongs to Raymond —

TON. He said he thought it was one of the kids'.

LYNNE. That's likely. Last day of school, for some of them — before the wide wide world. Final act of defiance.

TON. Defiance?

LYNNE. Motor-bikes not allowed in school.

TON (*lights another cigarette*). Decided . . . can't go on . . . this deception . . . lying . . . (*Pause.*) Hurting Carol . . .

LYNNE. Does she know about us? (*Pause.*) A suspicion?

TON. She's not stupid.

LYNNE. She married you.

TON. Thanks.

> *Pause.* TON *studies his feet.*

LYNNE. So . . . that's it. Fin. Arrivederci . . . dar . . . kaputt.

TON. Well, that's not exactly how I'd have put it. . .

LYNNE. But, that's it.

TON. It's Carol I'm thinking of. And the kids.

LYNNE. Oh well, thanks for having me.

TON. Look, we had . . . some pleasure . . . and — things end.

LYNNE. Funny, they do. Everything falls apart. One minute you love someone so badly you could tear out your innards for them. Another day you can pass them in the street and not feel a thing. Okay Ton. (*She sits on the bike.*)

TON. Look . . . I am sorry.

LYNNE. Yes.

TON. Now somehow . . . feel better, having put the record straight. Weight off my mind.

LYNNE. I'm pleased.

TON. Letting you know where you stand.

LYNNE. So . . . for example . . . in the staff-room. Carry on as if nothing happened? I mean — if you're getting stuck on the *Sun* crossword — should I assist or ignore you or — there's no bell.

TON. It's motorised, they have hooters. (*He sounds the horn.*)

LYNNE. So it does. I thought — (*She removes the petrol cap.*) — this . . .

TON. For Christ's sake! It's the petrol tank!

LYNNE. O.

TON. Cigarette burning — up in smoke.

He attempts to stub out his cigarette and replace the petrol cap simultaneously, and LYNNE slightly loses her balance; the result is they arrive in a clinch. They look at each other. He kisses her. Then stops.

Look, the match —

LYNNE. Ton, please, please —

She holds onto him as the door opens and the KID enters. Sixteen, but looks older. He speaks with a slight stutter not discernible until he is flustered. He is flustered by LYNNE and TON's embrace. TON glares at the KID.

TON. What you doing in here lad?

Pause.

LYNNE. I must —

She straightens her skirt. The KID takes it all in.

TON. What are you gaping at? You shouldn't be in here. Out of bounds. What are you doing in here?

KID. Me . . . bike . . . I . . .

TON. Yours?

KID. Me brother's . . .

TON. Rules, school rules. No motorised bikes. For pupils, not permitted, it's in the rules. And in here. This is a stockroom — not the Isle of Man TT.

Pause. Then:

KID. I . . . I'm leaving today. (*He smiles.*)

TON. That's no excuse.

Pause. Embarrassment. The KID is still trying to discover the cause of their embarrassment.

TON. You should be out on the playing field — to cheer the staff against the prefects.

KID. I was . . . going home.

TON. Not till after the final assembly.

KID. O.

LYNNE. I'd better —

TON. What are you gawking at lad? Hasn't anyone ever told you that it's rude to stare?

KID. Nar I —

TON. What are you staring at? Hmmm? And get this damned contraption out of here. Bunsen burners and chemicals and heaven knows what. Tank full of petrol. Go up. Come on, jump to it, chop chop.

The KID *attempts to take the bike but accidentally hits the pedals against* Ton's *shin. He yelps. Then, out of a mixture of fury and embarrassment, he clouts the* KID *round the head.*

KID. Ah!

TON. Bloody fool.

LYNNE. Ton!

The KID *and* TON *stare at each other; the* KID *holds his head.*

TON. Bloody idiot. And stop STARING!

Pause. TON *hits the* KID *again, harder.*

LYNNE. Ton, for God's sake leave him —

TON. He's gaping. Open-mouthed moron. (*He lights a cigarette.*) Yes, well . . . seemed to have closed his mouth. So lad, so you're leaving us today? (*Pause.*) Why not till the end of the summer term?

KID. I . . . I'm sixteen . . . now.

TON. I see. Look older . . . that your report?

KID. Yes . . .

TON. Weak . . . lazy . . . no aptitude . . . very poor . . . lazy . . . Well, you've certainly been consistent.

KID. Thank you.

LYNNE. What are you going to do?

Silence.

LYNNE. What job?

KID. Dunno . . . (*Pause.*) In here . . . you and her . . . (*He laughs quietly.*) Dirty old —

TON. SHUT UP.

The KID *sits on the bike.*

KID. Someone's nicked the top.

LYNNE. Here — (*She holds out the petrol cap.*)

KID. Very . . . d . . . d . . . dangerous. Light a fag over here and — (*He lights a cigarette and laughs at them. He is on the bike, close to the door. He closes the door, turns the key, pockets it.*)

TON. What the hell —

LYNNE. The door —

The KID *waves his cigarette over the petrol tank.*

KID. Gotcha!

TON *looks at* LYNNE.

TON. Now look here you bloody fool —

KID. Watchit.

TON. What's your name?

KID. Me name?

TON. What's his name?

LYNNE. What's . . . your name?

The KID *laughs.*

KID. You ask me me name? I've only been here five years!

TON *goes to him to get the key.*

TON. Now look here sonny, give me that key.

KID. Watchit. I'm . . . n . . . n . . . not messing . . . messing. (*He brandishes his fag and* TON *slowly retreats.*) Not, messing.

LYNNE. He isn't . . . whoever he is.

TON. Blow us all up would you?

KID. Give me one . . . one reason why not?

Pause.

LYNNE. Lots of reasons —

KID. Only asked for one.

TON. O Christ. (*He paces.*)

KID. Stay still —

TON. This is ridiculous.

KID. Still! You make me jittery. When you're jittery, that's when accidents happen.

LYNNE. The best way to avoid accidents is to —

KID. You can shut up and all. (*Pause.*) Fed up getting talked at, in't I. Told what to do, where to go, go there, come here, smash in the f . . . f . . . face. Up to here, wiv it. All for — well, that's the end of it. Today. Leaving, right. Five years here, ay. Into the unknown. Nothing . . .

LYNNE. Nothing . . .?

Silence.

KID. O, they've started the football match. STAY!

TON *has attempted to look out of the window. The* KID *makes him retreat.*

TON. You really would . . . do that? Have you any conception of the consequences of that action?

KID. Like what?

TON. You'd be expelled and no employer would touch you with a shitty finger-nail! A lifetime of —

KID. I thought you'd say — we'll all be killed.

TON. That, O yes.

KID. I doubt even Watling on a bad day'd expel a corpse. 'Look here . . . corpse . . . pull yourself together . . . and take that chewing gum out of yer mouth . . . what I have to say is very serious . . . pay attention . . . look alive . . .' (*He laughs.*) Funny smell . . . burning flesh . . . hangs in the air for ages . . .

He looks out of the window. LYNNE *and* TON *exchange a look.*

LYNNE. When you've finished . . . that cigarette . . . we'll all go, shall we?

Long silence.

I said when —

KID. Fancy screwing him. Great oaf . . . Do you know what we call him . . . Farty. That's what we call him, 'cause he keeps farting in the gym. So we call him Farty.

TON. You little bastard —

KID. Suits him, don't you think? Do you know why farts smell? For the benefit of the deaf.

Silence.

Good name, in't it. Farty.

Pause.

LYNNE. What's your name?

KID. I want you . . . I'm telling you . . . From now on, his name, officially is — Farty. Right? (*Pause.*) Say hello to him then. (*Pause.*) I'm warning you!

Pause.

LYNNE. Hello Farty.

The KID *laughs.*

KID. He's done it again! What a stink, what a scorcher! Whenever something makes him mad — he drops one. Cor, that was a terrible one!

LYNNE. Awful.

KID. Diabolical.

LYNNE. Appalling.

KID. Trench warfare — secret weapon — him.

LYNNE. O yes. (*She laughs.*)

TON. All right, Lynne . . . no need to . . . (*To the* KID.) Look here, that's enough. The game has gone on sufficiently to satisfy your end-of-school high jinks, now I propose —

KID. Farty!

TON. Listen, they're waiting for me out there. I've got a game of football to play. I'm right half!

KID. Ooooo.

TON. Miss Millar, I —

KID. Gorilla.

Pause.

LYNNE. What?

KID. Gorilla Millar, your name.

TON. Har har.

Silence.

KID. Good, in't it.

TON. O —

KID. Say hello to each other then. (*Pause.*) Go on, don't be shy. (*Pause.*) I ain't fucking joking!

TON. Hello, Gorilla.

LYNNE. Hello, Farty.

The KID *giggles, snorts, holds himself.*

TON. There, satisfied? Now can we please go?

KID. O no. Not yet. I mean to say, satisfied — well, satisfied is hardly the way I'm feeling. A very wrong word to use is satisfied. (*He looks out of the window.*) They've started the game without you Farty. Jenkins must have taken your place. The Billy Bonds of Botany.

TON. They'll be looking for me. Watling will have sent out search parties. My God, I'd hate to be in your shoes when they find you.

KID (*laughs again, turns to them*). In't it funny. Eh? What a scream. Farty is . . . scared. I can see it. Scared of me. You're sweating top of yer mouth . . . Forehead all red and thundery and . . . Years of shoving everyone around, slapping heads in the corridor, getting us giddy in the gym and doing every thing you like and now — Shitting yourself 'cause I got the power. Ain't I.

TON. You little . . . turd.

KID. Oooo, Betty. Naughty word . . . naughty . . . not nice.

TON. Shall I tell you why you're such a . . . stupid little sod, whatever your name is. Because you're short-sighted. That's why you're so stupid.

KID. That ain't my fault.

TON. Of course it is.

KID. I can't help it.

TON. Yes you can.

KID. Can't.

TON. Can.

KID. I can't help it, can I, Gorilla?

LYNNE. No . . . you can't help being stupid.

KID. Thank you. See.

TON. But you can help being short-sighted. You don't look further than your feet. Do you. Just look as far as your feet carry you. Live from day to day —

KID. I never plan that far ahead.

TON. You think you can call me . . . that word . . . and Miss Millar —

LYNNE. That word.

TON. Quiet, woman. Well, big laugh, very funny, o ho ho. But, but what afterwards, hmm? The consequences. What then?

Pause. The KID *lights a cigarette with hypnotising slowness.*

KID. What after today for me . . . anyhow . . . I've been here, getting prepared for today for . . . five years. The great day. Stepping out into the wide wide world, an' that. One of . . . how many kids here? Twelve hundred, eh. What's going to happen to this one here — (*He points at himself.*) — after today? Hmmm? Mmmm? Fifty years of working life is . . . all spread out in front of me . . . they say when you drown, in the last seconds before you go under, the whole of your life passes before your eyes . . . Well, this morning as we all stood there in the assembly, and the choir sang them hymns and the brass band blowed on their bugles and those clever bastards chanted out their bit of rhyme in Latin, an' that . . . and the mayor made his speech, so proud, so proud . . . and we all said them prayers to God Almighty . . . and we watched all them clever kids getting their prizes . . . clapping, clapping . . . going to university . . . clapping clapping . . . playing cricket for England. Boys in Pakistan . . . clapping clapping . . . well, me life didn't pass in front of me eyes . . . but me future did. A great mist of nothing . .-. (*Silence. He lights a cigarette. Looks out of the window.*) Pigeons sitting on the power cables . . . got it made, ain't they . . . can sit on power cables and not get burned . . . fly anywhere . . . grandad had em . . . funny, in't it . . . how pigeons don't sweat under their wings when they've been flying . . .

Pause.

TON. What do you want?

KID. Bonny! Want Bonny up here . . . in front of me . . . up here, down there . . . knees . . . make him sweat, make him bleed . . . blow him up! Know why he's called Bonny? Cause he keeps —

LYNNE. Asking everyone if they're *bona fide*?

KID. Right! Noticed that an' all? Noticed that, first thing I noticed when I came here, this lovely comprehensive. Him going up to the sixth formers and saying: Are you *bona fide* — 'bout university? About cricket tour, are you *bona fide*? I thought: 'Christ, what a lot of fucking brothers.' And then someone says, 'Nar — Latin, in't it. Means, serious.' An' I thought — told me brother and he said: 'Great school — great school, going round talking in Latin all day.' Great — that's the way to get your head smashed in in the factory, I think. (*Cool now.*) I want him, here. Bonny. I'm serious. See him?

TON. Yes . . .

KID. Call him then, go on!

TON (*at the window*). Mr Watling. Headmaster.

KID. Bonny!

TON. Yes, ah — up here. The science stockroom.

KID. Close it.

TON *closes the window.*

He coming?

TON. Yes . . .

KID. Well, in't this nice and cosy?

> *Blackout. Crash in Stones'* Get Off Of My Cloud.

Scene Two

Music continues, fades out before lights come up.
Knocking on the door.
Lights up to reveal: the KID *on bike;* LYNNE *and* TON *anxious.*
The knocking continues.

VOICE (*off*). Mr Peart, are you there?

> *The* KID *nods that* TON *should reply.*

TON. Yes, I'm here.

VOICE (*off*). Then, open the door.

TON. I . . . I'm . . . we're in a bit of a jam.

> *Pause.*

VOICE (*off*). A what?

TON. There's a kid here — gone berserk.

> *The* KID *laughs.*

VOICE (*off*). Who's there?

KID. Listen Bonny. D'yer wanna come in?

VOICE (*off*). Open this door.

KID. Ask nicely.

VOICE (*off*). OPEN THIS DOOR IMMEDIATELY.

> *The* KID *giggles.*

KID. Well, if you ain't gonna ask nicely, you ain't gonna come
in. Fair's fair.

VOICE (*off*). What is going on in there?

TON. We're . . . sort of hostages.

VOICE (*off*). Who is with you?

TON. Miss Millar and — a lad.

VOICE (*off*). Who is it?

KID (*whispers*). King.

TON (*loud*). His name is King.

KID. Arthur.

TON. Arthur. (*He glares at the* KID *, who laughs.*)

VOICE (*off*). Open this door at once!

KID. Say please.

TON. I think, headmaster —

LYNNE. It does appear . . . serious.

   Pause.

VOICE (*off*). Let me in . . . please.

KID. I can't hear him, can you?

TON. I —

KID. Louder, Bonny. Farty here's breathing so heavy I can't hear you.

VOICE (*off*). Please. Let me in.

KID. Please.

VOICE (*off*). Please.

KID. Coming to something when I have to teach a headmaster his manners, like. Didn't no-one teach you no manners? Still can't hear you, tell you what . . . gap under the door. Talk through that — might hear yer then.

VOICE (*off*). Wait there Mr Peart — I'll get the caretaker, master key —

   The KID *holds his cigarette closer to the petrol tank and screams.*

KID. I ain't fucking joking!

TON. You fool — close to the fumes — get it away from the fumes — don't you know too close to the fumes and, accidentally —

KID. Makes it exciting, dunnit! Get him in here. I want him in here.

LYNNE. I think, headmaster . . . before things slip out of hand —

TON. Tragedy —

LYNNE. It would be best if you do what —

KID. King Arthur —

LYNNE. Says.

Pause.

VOICE (*from the gap under the door*). Please let me come in.

Pause.

KID. Right. Action stations. Put out the red carpet — stand to attention, hats off for the queen. (*He gestures* LYNNE *to stand close to him. He holds her hair above the tank with one hand and the cigarette with the other.*) Him in. You try anything and I ain't kidding — we're all blood and bone on the ceiling, right! (*He puts his hand up* LYNNE's *skirt.*)

TON. You filthy little bastard.

KID. What does it say on Durex machines?

TON. I —

KID. Shut up.

LYNNE. I don't know. What does it say on Durex machines?

KID. Buy me and stop one. Heeeeee. O, that's nice . . . exciting.

TON rages.

So what. I'm in charge now Farty. Your time is up. Go dance on . . . go crunch egg-shells now. Here's the key. Open up and let him in and lock it and key back to me and try anything and I break a bottle in her cunt. Right.

This is done gingerly. The door opens and we find the head-master on his knees. He enters.

HEAD. Oh, I see . . .

KID. Shut it. Door.

TON shuts the door, gives the KID *the key. Silence. The* KID *gropes her more.*

HEAD. Remove your hand. I take your point.

KID. Bollocks. She likes it. (*Then he releases her. She wipes her watering eyes. Adjusts her dress.*)

The three adults look at each other.

HEAD. I have no idea what precisely you think you are playing at, but I give you warning, the repercussions are going to be exceedingly serious.

KID. *Bona fide?*

   Pause.

TON. He's, he's — threatening to.

   The KID *lights a cigarette.*

HEAD. There is a very strict rule in this school preventing pupils smoking on the premises.

KID. Nice one.

TON. He's threatening to . . . set off the petrol.

KID. Right.

LYNNE. Please . . . please . . .

HEAD. What do you hope to . . . what do you think you're going to achieve by this? Err, Johnson isn't it?

KID. No.

HEAD. Raynor —

KID. No.

HEAD. Ansell —

KID. Pass.

   Pause

HEAD. Do you know him?

TON. I think . . . I've seen him about the school.

HEAD. Miss Millar?

LYNNE. I recognise . . . him, but —

HEAD. Neither of you knows his name?

LYNNE. No.

HEAD. I see.

TON. It's an . . . awfully big school, headmaster —

HEAD. I am aware of that.

TON. Can't be expected to know the names of all twelve hundred —

HEAD. I am interested only in *his* name. Well, boy? This has gone on far long enough. What's your name?

KID. It's on me report.

TON. Ah yes! He had his report.

HEAD. He's shown it to you?

TON. Yes.

HEAD. What name was on it?

Pause.

TON. Ah, I didn't actually notice —

HEAD. And you, Miss Millar?

LYNNE. No, I didn't.

Pause.

HEAD. Okay lad. Let's see it. If you are not prepared to tell us your name, let me read it —

KID. No.

HEAD. I see no —

KID. No. It's mine. My property. I mean, like the way I gathered . . . this report here in me pocket, it's what I show the employment exchange, an' that — to get a job. And all them things you lot . . . teachers . . . written on it. Well, way I see it, none of them didn't exactly do me a favour. None of that gonna help me much — specially what *you* wrote. Head-master's comment, at the bottom, God's word, the big deal — the final sentence, end of trial — judge's verdict. (*Pause.*) Achieved little here . . . not a success . . . (*Pause.*) That's what you wrote, an' signed it an' — (*Slight pause.*) An' now you tell me you don't know who the fuck I am!

Silence.

HEAD. Then you tell me who you are.

KID. Ahhha. Listen, way I see it, I reckon you oughta found out who this geezer here was before you started putting in the boot. Not a success, weak, lazy, no aptitude no achievement an' — lovely signature tho'.

HEAD. I cannot reasonably be expected to know everyone here. I have to rely upon the opinions of the other members of my staff . . . who do know the pupils.

KID. What, him? Farty there? He don't know me from Adam. And her? She don't know me? An' you don't. I'm the only bleeder here who knows who I am!

HEAD. This is all . . . rather beside the point.

KID (*to* LYNNE). Give us a kiss.

LYNNE. I'd rather not.

KID. If you play your cards right, I'll let you have a suck.

HEAD. This . . . gratuitous crudity —

KID. Kissus.

LYNNE. Let me see your report first.

KID (*in a child's voice*). If I show you my report will you show me what's under your knickers?

TON *has moved towards him.*

Hold it, Farty — far enough, no more! Christ, how many more times! I ain't kiddin' you know! This is . . . for real. This is, it. Ever seen what happens when you walk through a fire?

Pause.

HEAD. Was all this . . . a premeditated rebellion?

KID. You what?

HEAD. Was all this — premeditated?

KID. Come again?

HEAD. I asked —

LYNNE. Did you plan this?

KID. O. (*He lights a cigarette.*)

HEAD. If it was unplanned, let us stop it now and forget all about a momentary lapse . . . a slight madness of the moment.

KID. O . . . O . . . runs in the family. Me grandmum was mad. Ol' grandma. Round the bleedin' bend, she went. They locked her up. In a room no bigger than this. I used to go and see her. She sat in the garden. And peeled chestnuts and buried orange pips in the grass. I said to her: 'Why are you here?' She said: 'They say I'm mad.' I said, 'Why's that?' She says: ''Cause I go up the shops with no clothes on.' I said: 'Don't you feel cold?' 'Nar,' she says, 'I only do it in heat-waves.'

Pause.

LYNNE. You liked her?

KID. Me gran?

LYNNE. Yes . . . ?

KID. Course I did, everyone loves their grans.

LYNNE. Did she die?

KID. Mind your own.

LYNNE. Just interest.

KID. She used to wet the bed . . . so they had to take her away. She kept wetting the bed.

LYNNE. Was she very old?

KID. Dunno . . . She seemed a hundred, but I was younger. She said to me brother: 'If you ain't in bed by ten o'clock, come home.' (*He laughs.*)

LYNNE laughs; the KID laughs more. The HEAD laughs; TON makes out he is laughing. Slowly, they stop laughing.

KID. I never got it.

Pause.

TON. This is all fantastically interesting but isn't it about time —

HEAD. Jolly interesting indeed. Your grandmother sounds a most remarkable woman.

KID. You should have heard her sing!

HEAD. I would . . . very much like to have heard her sing.

KID. Duke's Head, that's where she sang.

HEAD. Ah, in the High Street —

KID. An' played the piano. Johanna. She had this johanna at home. An' every Christmas, when we was kids, we'd go there and she'd play the johanna. An' every Christmas, just before Christmas, she'd paint it — you know, with that wood-dye stuff an' then the room'd hot up, you know, everyone there, singing an' that. And me old man'd say . . . Well, see — he'd put his beer glass on top of the piano while they was all singing an' that — and all the fellahs'd try and get their glasses off the piano — (*He mimes it.*) But — they'd have been stuck there 'cause the wood-dye was tacky, you know! Laugh!

HEAD. Home entertainments.

KID. Yeah.

HEAD. Rarely one hears a piano nowadays.

KID. Except in assembly.

HEAD. Not the same thing.

KID. It ain't.

HEAD. Not like the self entertainment of closely knit working class families, the simple pleasures, the warm feel of —

KID. She stopped wetting the bed.

HEAD. An advancement —

KID. An' shit in it instead. So, they locked her up. (*Pause.*) Stupid thing to do. The lav was a half mile walk away.

The HEAD *is passing a message with his eyes to* LYNNE *during all this, as the* KID *looks out of the window.*

Close, should have scored. The prefects' keeper — he's a wanker. Talk about let a ball through his legs — a bleeding oil tanker could get through his legs.

HEAD. Are you all right, Miss Millar?

LYNNE. Just a bit . . . claustrophobic.

HEAD. You look . . . unwell . . .

LYNNE. It's . . . my time, you know.

HEAD. Ah, you had better — sit down . . .

LYNNE. Yes, I —

HEAD. Mr Peart —

TON. O. Yes —

HEAD. The stool for Miss Millar —

TON. Ah —

HEAD. I think she's going to faint —

During the confusion of LYNNE *staggering and* TON *getting the stool and passing it to the* HEAD, *the* KID *loses his concentration, and* TON *makes a grab for his cigarette. But the* KID *knocks* TON *off balance and screams.*

KID. YOU TRICKING BASTARDS! Right. You've fucking had it now. Stay there Farty, don't get up, lay down. That's it. Right. Okay. Fags outa pockets, right. Fast. I'm warning you.

TON *removes his cigarettes.*

An' yours.

The HEAD *slowly hands him his cigarettes — across the floor.*

Right. (*The* KID, *panting, wipes his forehead.*) Stay . . . stay there Farty.

TON. This is — insanity!

KID. No-one's asking you.

TON. Madness.

KID. You should know, you're a bleeding loon.

TON. If you aren't careful, your stupidity will become a severe handicap to you.

KID. Shut up! Stop . . . m . . m . . mixing me up. I'm . . . I'm all on me own up here!

Silence.

Understand that.

TON. I understand all right, Sonny Jim. All of you — all endless provocations!

KID. Bastard!

TON. Little shit.

KID. An' you can stop laughing an' all.

LYNNE. I'm not laughing . . . I'm not. I feel . . . sad for you, your loneliness.

KID. I got hundreds of mates. Send 'em up here, I will. Do you over.

LYNNE. Yes. I deserve it, I'm sure.

KID. Dirty trick, that was — filthy, disgusting.

LYNNE. I do . . . feel faint.

KID. You said you was on.

LYNNE. I do feel faint.

KID. Bit different. Have you doing handstands.

LYNNE. Why not cartwheels?

KID. Not enough room, or I would.

LYNNE. Shame.

KID. Preaching morality at us . . . all day. What to do. Having it off with this pig here. Married, in't he. That's not what you teach us.

LYNNE. I don't think it is really any of your business.

KID. I see right through you.

LYNNE. You don't have to be . . . alone.

KID. Don't try an' butter me up —

TON. Waste of bloody butter.

KID. Okay Farty, keep you quiet. Fifty press-ups.

TON. Fifty!

KID. Fifty!

TON. I'm not doing no fifty —

KID. You made Henry do fifty and he had a boil under his arm.

TON. Ah, so you're one of Henry's mob are you? The choc ice and vinegar crisps luncheon club.

KID (kicks him). Move.

TON. If it makes you feel very big . . . (Begins press-ups.)

HEAD. I'm . . . sorry.

  Pause.

KID. That's better.

HEAD. I meant, I'm sorry but I simply don't understand what you are hoping to achieve.

KID. Ah ha. Ha ha. I've heard that one before.

HEAD. What —

KID. Don't tell me, I'll get it . . . it'll come to me . . . achieve . . . achieve — I know! The school motto!

HEAD. The what?

KID. No, your signature tune? Yeah! Okay, I don't get it. Give us another clue.

HEAD. What are you talking about?

KID. Here, in this place, everyone's so busy ACHIEVING, everything else is . . . invisible.

  Pause.

LYNNE. I think he is trying to say? . . .

KID. What am I trying to say?

LYNNE. Do you mean —

KID. You've got . . . terrific eyes, you know . . .

LYNNE. Are you saying, your apparent . . . lack of success at school —

KID. Success! That's the other word, like that word . . . knocks me out that word. Oh here — there's a lot of it about.

LYNNE. And you . . . sense an awareness . . . that you have been unable to compete on those terms although —

KID. What the bleedin' hell are you talking about darling?

TON *stops doing press-ups.*

TON. Don't humour the sod, Lynne.

KID. Keep your arse down Farty, I can see your brains moving.

TON. Headmaster, really — isn't it about time that —

KID. I said, fifty.

TON. I did fifty.

KID. No, you never.

TON. You weren't counting.

KID. Start again, an' I'll count this time.

TON. That's not fair!

KID. Too bad.

TON. I've had enough of this.

KID. Your hard luck.

TON. Listen boy, when this little game is over —

KID. Oh yeah, go on go on go on, tell me!

TON's *rage becomes hysterical.*

TON. When you've burned your silly little weedy fingers with your silly little matches —

KID. Whey, hey!

TON. Then I shall be fully entitled to do what normally I am not permitted to do —

KID (*holds his nose*). Cor, what a scorcher!

TON. You are the basest —

KID. Open the bull gates —

TON. Snivelling, snot-stained —

KID. Fight! Fight!

TON. There is a stench of second-classness in this room which is positively nauseating. Everything about you — puny, spotty, skinny —

KID. Oi oi.

TON. Second-class, second-rate — that's you. No bloody hoper.

KID. I like it. I like it.

TON. There's only one thing this sort of herbert understands —

HEAD. Really, Mr Peart, control yourself!

TON. You can't argue with them, headmaster. You can't be rational with the irrational —

HEAD. Mr Peart, you are not helping the situation!

TON. I am not interested in helping yobboes like this one. I am interested in decency and endeavour and — order. He is disorder.

HEAD. Let us talk —

TON. But it's a waste of time talking to someone like him. Words don't have meaning with people like — Kung Fu in the playground and sick notes on the playing field. He can only mock, he cannot do. And whine and complain. And leer. Look at him, headmaster. Leering. Make no mistake, headmaster, that is a leer if ever I saw one, a chromium-plated leer.

KID. I'm only here for the leer.

TON. Little shits. No good wasting words on him; not a word in the ear of this one, only thing he'll understand is a kick in the balls, mate. (*Screaming.*) He's the sort of boyo who's never done fifty press-ups in his life! And . . . he's scared, oh yes, scared, scared . . . more terrified than he's ever been in his life, because this time he's gone too far . . . too, too far and he knows it and he's terrified.

Pause.

KID. But I ain't the one who's shaking. (*He laughs, slightly hysterically.*)

TON. Go on, laugh, laugh. That's all you can do. Mock, snigger, and whine afterwards. That's you, I know you. The shadows who never have showers, never do games, never do anything except march round the school in gangs, kicking doors, disrupting lessons, picking fights and jeering outside the staffroom. Do you know what you need? You need castrating! If you had any sense you'd know what castrating means and so you wouldn't laugh. Because in a little while you'll be babbling incoherent apologies at my knees and I'll kick your fucking head in!

Silence.

KID. Finding out m . . m . . more a . . b . . b . . bout him than me. O . . . suddenly . . . feel brass monkey . . .

LYNNE. You're shivering . . .

KID. Cold in here . . . sudden, all of a . . . cold . . .

LYNNE. Let us go out, out into the sun.

KID. Gives me headaches, sun . . . don't like the sun, much . . . runs in the family . . . 'Welcome to the Birds Eye country . . .'

LYNNE. What's that mean?

KID. Summer adverts . . . fields an' flowers an' . . . summer pisses me off, you know.

Pause.

HEAD. Would you mind awfully if I had a cigarette?

KID. What was that?

HEAD. I said —

KID. Funny noise. Are the radiators playing up? Could have sworn I heard sommat.

HEAD. I said would you —

KID. You still here. Christ. Still! You know, you're onto a winner here. Other jobs, factories an' 'at — missing five minutes and they dock yer pay. You been here half an hour and no-one realises you've been gone.

HEAD. Oh, they will.

KID. Reckon?

HEAD. I most certainly do.

KID. I don't. I reckon everyone's having a so lovely time. No you pacing about the corridors, hammering doors, disrupting lessons and kinda picking fights. Sticking yer hooter in where you ain't welcome.

HEAD. May I . . . please? . . . have one of my cigarettes.

KID. Ah, o no . . . no chance. I mean, might need that one. The one I give you might be me last one. Saving it, for the big bang.

HEAD. Very well then. Perhaps you will . . . at least enlighten me. What is this all about?

KID. I ain't messin' about.

HEAD. I believe you. You have convinced me of that. But, I would very much like to know what —

KID. Come in here, for the motor — saw them, at it. O, got this pain in me head . . . behind me eyes . . . started! This . . . did . . .

HEAD. An unpremeditated chain of events began which . . . will end where?

Silence.

Well?

KID. D . . d . . dunno, sir.

Silence.

Don't ask me questions . . .

HEAD. Then think about it. We can't stay here forever. Soon, you'll be getting hungry.

KID. No trouble. Shout out the window. Tell them to send in food for us. Tons of it. Anything we want, they'll send it in. Like the Balcombe Street thingy. From the cafe, piping hot. Chips an' that. Soup. Surprised the old-age pensioners ain't started it. Say they're held prisoners in their flats an' that. Get the cops to rush 'em up grub. Cut the cost of living, they'd live like kings. No charge, see. Chicken and chips an' —

LYNNE. Roast beef!

KID. Oh yeah, an' tons of spuds —

LYNNE. Roasted —

KID. No way different. Lamb chops and sausages an' hot dogs —

LYNNE. Pizzas —

KID. Salami and onion, pepperoni special —

LYNNE. Don't get that school dinners.

KID. You're making me feel hungry.

LYNNE. I am.

Pause.

KID. What you doing with a nutter like him?

She shrugs.

'Cause, you ain't so bad looking.

Pause.

LYNNE. Too skinny.

KID. Nar, just right.

LYNNE. Bones, all bones.

KID. It's the right look now.

LYNNE. No. (*She gestures towards her breasts.*)

KID. Overrated, them are . . . as long as there's sommat there.

LYNNE. O, they're there —

KID. That's all right then.

LYNNE. Not much but —

KID. Bums.

LYNNE. Beg your pardon?

KID. Bums. Bum man, me.

TON. Bloody queer.

KID. You can shut up. I've had enough of you, Peart, I'm
talking to the lady. So . . . you like bums?

HEAD. I . . . do not dislike them.

KID. Herrrrrrr.

Slight pause.

LYNNE. Do you have a girlfriend?

Pause.

KID. Ah ha.

LYNNE. All right, I'm sorry. It has nothing to do with me.

KID. Make you laugh, years ago this was, me brother got sent home from junior school with a letter saying he'd been sent home for touching up Peggy Highsmith's tits. Me dad, this was when he was living at home, see — he says to Roy: 'That's really disgusting Roy, I'm ashamed of you. When I was your age I'd have had me hands in her quim.' (*He laughs.*)

TON. You'd need a bloody compass, to find it.

KID. If he don't shut up I'll lip him.

TON. O yes? I doubt it. But I do know that I'm going to take that cigarette out of your hand —

KID. Then you'd better move fast Farty. (*He holds it over the petrol tank.*) Okay. This is it. Count of ten. Ten, nine, eight, seven, six, five . . . say yer prayers . . . four, three, two, one —

The HEAD *faces the door.* LYNNE *closes her eyes. Then* TON *closes his eyes. The* KID *drops a huge rack of test-tubes on the floor. Smash! He screams with laughter. Slowly, they recover from their fear.*

LYNNE. Very clever. Very good, very convincing. Sure fooled us.

The KID *lights a new cigarette.*

KID. Yeah.

HEAD. You have made a . . . point of sorts. What do you want?

KID. What a question!

HEAD. I'm sorry if it appears perverse, but —

KID. Watch your bleeding language.

HEAD. What is all this . . . spectacle . . . supposed to mean?

KID. You're twitching.

HEAD. Ah.

KID. A definite twitch.

HEAD. I'm getting rather tired.

KID. You've got rather a long day. Match this morning, end of term assembly this afternoon and dance for the sixth form tonight, their dance, don't forget that.

HEAD. What do you want of us?

KID. Oh yeah, a lot of talking you've got on today. Oh yeah.
One thing I've always wondered — you don't mind me asking
do you? Well, I've always wondered — do you get as bored
talking as we do listening?

Pause.

HEAD. Mr Peart, as you are nearest to the window, perhaps you'd
try to raise the alarm.

TON. Ah, yes.

KID. Oi —

HEAD. But I presume this entire drama is some obscure attempt
to draw attention to yourself . . . Thus, by raising the alarm,
Mr Peart will be assisting in your cause.

KID. You don't arf get on me tits when you talk like that.

HEAD. Like . . . what?

KID. Bored . . . weary voice . . . you know, seen it all before . . .

HEAD. As a matter of fact, I do rather find all this . . . boring.
It's a waste of time.

KID. My five years here have been a waste of time.

LYNNE. Have they?

KID. For a teacher, you can't arf be thick.

LYNNE. I do my best.

KID. It ain't fucking good enough!

HEAD. For . . . you?

KID. Don't be smug, Bonny, don't sneer, don't piss all over me.
A couple of minutes ago you was shitting yourself.

HEAD. You are deluding yourself, boy.

KID. I could see it . . . in your eyes . . . I can see what you think.
It's in your eyes . . . First day here . . . lined up in front of
you, all hundreds of us — the new kids. Lined up in the playground . . . all of us in lines and you wandering along, eyes
flickering over us . . . deciding who's doing what, who's going
where. Flick of the eyes . . . he's got a nice jacket. Clean
trousers and starched handkerchief . . . O levels for him. Like
Farty says, you see the no-hopers . . . relegate them. Out of
the way.

He takes a long drag on his cigarette.

Listen to your chat, speech-day — mayor there . . . talking.
About how proud he is of this school, this everso terrific
comprehensive school . . . the big, big, school . . . everyone all
together . . . all chances, hundreds of subjects, something for
everyone, put out your hand and take what you want —
But . . . watched your eyes . . . not even looking at the poor
sod of a mayor. 'Humour him,' your eyes said. 'Humour him.
Dreamer!'

He sighs. Pause.

Now . . . found out . . . I was right. Comprehensive! (*He spits.*)
Me brother, me brother wow, what he said about it when I
come here! Chance for you, kiddo, he said to me. Secondary
school he went to. No hope. Chucked in there. Factory fodder,
but this comprehensive! Paradise. So different he said . . . and
he supposed to know. Knows the mayor, delivered his leaflets
for him at elections, me brother did. Knew all about what was
gonna happen in this new school. This is your big chance,
kiddo, he says . . .

Pause.

Got it wrong. Just the same. Only bigger. Anything you want
here, they said. Yeah. If you're clever, if you're bright, big
hope . . . glittering prizes! Just the same, as it was for me
brother . . . just . . . the same. Only bigger. Achievement . . .
successes . . . only way it's judged . . . all them O levels, all
them A levels, all them clever bastards going to university.
What a clever headmaster, what a smashing lot a teachers, what
a great school. What a fantastic school — What about us? Who
don't do O levels? What about me, eh? How good is this?

*He throws the report on the floor. Stamps on it. Stands
breathing deeply.*

HEAD. It is . . . never easy to build a perfect world . . . a new
Jerusalem in Rainham. . . It's a gradual process, slow steps . . .
making a net of tighter mesh . . . it takes time.

KID. Time, I do not have. Only . . . one life.

HEAD. Even so, every opportunity has been afforded to you
here. If you have some grievance —

KID. You don't even know me name!

HEAD. You won't tell me.

KID. You should find out.

HEAD. You must help yourself.

KID. That's your get-out, in't it. Help yourself — help yourself — and if you *can't* help yourself — then it's your own fucking fault.

Pause.

LYNNE. What do you, want to do?

KID. He said . . . they all said here — EVERYTHING'S possible. On the threshold of . . . everything you want.

LYNNE. What do you want?

KID. Bit late in the day . . .

HEAD. For God's sake — you're only 16.

KID. Still time?

They are encouraged by this change of tack.

HEAD. A lifetime before you . . .

KID. Do . . . anything . . . aye?

HEAD. Within your capabilities.

KID. I thought the idea here was to 'expand' them.

HEAD. Yes, yes — that is the premise upon which —

KID (*waving his cigarette near the petrol*). I wanna blow you up, *Bonny.*

HEAD. Mr Peart, are you having any —

KID. Wanna see you — up there, up there — bits of limb all bloody hanging down like decorations.

TON (*at the window, with urgency*). Up here, up here!

KID. I've had enough of you, you pompous git. (*He grabs the* HEAD *by his neck. The* HEAD *whimpers. The* KID *holds the* HEAD's *face above the petrol tank.*) Get away from that window, I ain't pissing now, one false move Farty and he's smoke.

HEAD. Ah, ah, ah.

LYNNE. All right — you've made your point. What do you want us to do?

KID. That's better.

LYNNE. What do you want of us?

KID. Help me . . . he . . . lp mmmmme. Make a life . . . Help me
. . . m . . m . . (*His stutter defeats him. Now he is weeping.*)
Get a . . . job . . . not factory, not like me brother, all gone
grey and old and white . . . and 'at . . . a job . . .

LYNNE. If it's a job you want —

KID. Nice job . . . car and that.

LYNNE. We'll help all we can, of course we will.

KID (*points to the* HEAD). He's the one gotta help.

HEAD. I . . . shall.

KID. 'Cause I'm a pupil an' all that.

HEAD. Yes.

KID. Anything's possible, you said.

HEAD. Yes.

KID. Lying bleeder.

HEAD. No, no — it is.

KID. Well then!

HEAD. Well then, what?

KID. Promise.

HEAD. I p . . p . . promise, I do.

KID. Honest.

HEAD. Aaaaaaah. Fumes . . . choking me.

LYNNE. You're choking him, you fool.

TON. For Christ's sake —

KID. You gotta promise —

TON. For God's sake be careful —

HEAD. I promise!

KID. Me, a job that —

HEAD. Yes, yes, YES!

KID. I want a job . . . a job that — (*He releases the* HEAD
gingerly.) You said, work hard — everything possible.

HEAD. If . . . you are prepared to work hard . . .

KID. Make it possible, make it happen.

HEAD. Yes . . .

    Pause.

KID. I want . . . to be . . . a brain surgeon.

    Pause.

TON. I'll risk it, I will kill him.

KID. You said! (*Pause.*) Promise is a promise.

TON. He's taking the piss in the most devious way —

HEAD. Did you say, you wished to become —

KID. I always wanted to be a brain surgeon . . . Doctor Casey . . . Car he had, and bints! O, yeah . . . you said here, anything possible.

TON. I'll take a chance, no-one'll know —

    Pause. TON retreats.

KID. Well? You promised —

HEAD. It's not . . . impossible. Not beyond the most remote bounds of . . . possibility. If you work hard.

TON. Headmaster!

HEAD. Be quiet.

LYNNE. But headmaster.

HEAD. Silence! Boy here, vocation — a vocation, is it boy?

KID. Yeah.

HEAD. Like science, do you?

KID. Never done it.

TON. Like offals do you?

HEAD. Shut up, Mr Peart. Nothing more natural in the world than . . . a boy with spirit, dedication . . . not unintelligent, evening classes, hard work . . . could achieve . . . qualifications I see no reason why . . . shouldn't . . . give it time . . . patience, hard work . . . oh yes, eventually, medical school . . . become a doctor —

KID. I said, brain surgeon —

HEAD. A doctor first —

KID I dunno about that.

HEAD. I think, the best way —

KID. All right then, I'll take your advice.

HEAD. Good. Doctor, then specialise.

KID. On brains.

HEAD. Quite.

KID. So, it's possible?

HEAD. Probable.

KID. Even though, I never did no exams here, no CSE's or —

HEAD. O, I think qualifications are somewhat overrated, you know —

KID. Yerr, here — have a fag.

HEAD. One thinks of Shakespeare . . . Churchill . . . men who achieved, succeeded without the advantage of . . . CSE's.

He laughs, the KID *laughs.* TON *is furious.*

KID. Churchill eh.

HEAD. Not a success at school. Nor Milton nor Van Gogh nor —

KID. Andy Fairweather-Low?

HEAD. Proves my point. Great shortage of brain surgeons.

KID. Specially ones without any CSE's.

HEAD. Always in demand. Excellent career prospects.

KID. Great.

HEAD. But, have to work hard.

KID. Some people'd say — what you're telling me, all a dream. A load of crap to keep me quiet.

HEAD. Ah —

KID. But you wouldn't lie to me, would you — wouldn't tell the kids here — the ones who ain't no good at nothing — you wouldn't raise their hopes would you when you didn't mean what you was saying.

HEAD. Certainly not. Dreams materialise here . . . if you work hard, study hard, apply yourself — application and —

KID. Be a brain surgeon.

HEAD. You shall be a brain surgeon if that is what you want.

KID. And play for West Ham.

>Pause.

>Striker.

>TON *explodes.*

TON. Him! He doesn't know a fucking goal-post from an elm tree. He's never done two successive games lessons in his five years here! He can't play football.

HEAD. Really Mr Peart, you go too far. There are . . . lots of professional footballers who, apparently, lacked ability on the school playing field — to the undiscerning eye . . . I see no reason why what's 'isname here shouldn't make a first class professional footballer for West Ham. If he applies himself.

KID. And be a brain surgeon.

HEAD. Indeed.

>*They all nod seriously. The* KID *giggles then hysterically.*

KID. Cunts.

>*Blackout. Stones'* Street Fighting Man, *loud.*

Scene Three

The same night.
The Beatles' Here Comes The Sun.
Police cars' blue swirling lights off. The HEAD *and* TON *are asleep on the floor in a corner.* LYNNE *sits in the centre watching the* KID, *who has his shirt wide open, his tie off, and is sweating. He is smoking and leaning against the wall beside the bike. A long silence, just the music.*

KID. All them cops . . . and people . . . and dogs . . . all looking up here. (*Pause.*) I like this song.

LYNNE. The Beatles.

KID. Do you remember the Beatles?

LYNNE. God, you make me sound old.

KID. I heard me brother talk about them. Had their records. Originals, not the re-releases. Funny, in't it. Me mum loves them now. *Yesterday* and that. When they first come out she used to hate them.

LYNNE. Do you think your mum and dad are still down there?

KID. Dunno. Don't care.

LYNNE. Don't you get on with them then?

KID. Why the fuck did they have to come?

LYNNE. Perhaps they . . . just want you to go home with them?

KID. I ain't going anywhere.

LYNNE. What do you think's going to happen when the cigarettes run out?

KID. We might all be dead by then . . .

LYNNE. But you're only sixteen. You don't want to die, do you? I don't want to die yet. How old do you think I am?

KID. Dunno.

LYNNE. Guess.

KID. Ninety-three.

LYNNE. Cheeky sod.

KID. About twenty-five . . . twenty-six.

LYNNE. About that . . . does that sound old to you?

KID. Not old, is it. Me brother's older than that.

LYNNE. The one who delivers leaflets for the Labour Party.

KID. He did, before he moved.

LYNNE. And you've got a gran, who's . . . mad?

KID. Nar . . . she's dead.

Pause.

LYNNE. *Liked* her . . .

KID. Yeah, I liked her . . . a lot. An' me grandad . . . smart, he was. White silk scarf, tied in a knot . . . old suit . . . but always wore his scarf . . . raced his pigeons . . . put on his suit and tied his scarf and we'd go up to the Fife to deliver the pigeons for the race on a Friday night, you know . . . and Saturday afternoons . . . in the summer . . . waiting in his yard, smoking . . . and talking an' that . . . sun shining . . . waiting . . . for the pigeons to come home. An' one day I said to him,

said — how do they know where to come back to? An' he
looked at me, an' he said: It's the homing instinct . . . in the
end, everyone has to come home.

*Pause. He wearily lights another cigarette. New Record: From
Rod Stewart's* Atlantic Crossing, This Old Heart of Mine *and*
Sailing.

Good bloke he was . . . me grandad . . . no-one promised him
nothing. No-one sold him dreams that weren't gonna happen.
So he was happy. With what he got. (*Pause.*) Know what I
mean . . .? (*Pause.*) O, this pain . . . in me head. (*Pause.*) Christ.
(*He slumps to the floor holding his head.*) Rod Stewart.

LYNNE. Yeah.

KID. Like this, slow side better than the fast side. Never play
the fast side. Me brother liked the fast side, but now he's gone,
never play it.

LYNNE. I prefer this side.

KID. He took me to see the Faces once . . . at the Rainbow.
Queued and queued we did. Got tickets. Went . . . an' it was
the night of the bleeding power cuts. No wonder they voted
Heath out.

She laughs gently.

LYNNE. Good enough reason.

KID. They akip or what?

LYNNE. Exhausted, hungry . . .

KID. I beat 'em.

LYNNE. Yes, you did.

KID. I ain't tired, ain't hungry.

LYNNE. No-o-o . . .

KID. Funny . . . downstairs . . . they're all still dancing an'
outside — cops with cars an' dogs an' that.

LYNNE. Life doesn't stop because . . .

KID. What?

LYNNE. Can you dance?

KID. Leave off. (*He looks out of the window.*) All them, for me.

Silence. He lights another cigarette.

LYNNE. You've only got three cigarettes left.

KID. So?

LYNNE. An observation.

KID. I ain't stupid.

LYNNE. No, you're not.

KID. Ain't clever neither.

LYNNE. I'm not sure . . .

KID. Other people, they get by 'cause they're clever, like Bonny
wants 'em to be . . . or good at games like Farty . . . what
about . . . me?

LYNNE. Other things.

KID. Yeah, but they don't count.

LYNNE. They do.

KID. How could you go with him?

LYNNE. I don't want . . . always to be on my own . . .

KID. Nar, nor did I . . .

Silence.

What's gonna happen to me . . . what I've done?

Pause.

I said, what's —

LYNNE. I don't know . . . don't know, wish I did, could do —
I just don't know.

KID. Shouldn't promise things what you don't mean. That's more
wrong than what I done. Achieve, succeed — that pisses me
off. But it's what counts, don't it. Trouble is, if you know you
ain't achieving, makes it hard. OK if you dunno.

LYNNE. Look. (*Pause.*) What you mustn't do . . . (*Pause.*) Them,
don't judge yourself by their standards . . .

*Long silence. Then the KID hits the bike, suddenly turns to
her.*

KID. Dance then?

*They begin to jive. He stops. She strokes his hair; trembling,
he begins to cry. She holds him. The KID breaks down.
Slowly TON rises and grabs the KID savagely. Holds him down.*

TON. You bleeder — shit — I'll fucking —

LYNNE. Ton, leave him alone — can't you see he's been through enough —

TON. I'll bloody —

HEAD. Well done Miss Millar, congratulations. A very clever move.

LYNNE. I d . . didn't mean THAT. It wasn't a trap — (*She screams.*)

   TON *has the* KID *on the floor.*

HEAD (*at the window*). Siege over!

   Voices. Blue lights go off. The music stops.

LYNNE. I didn't mean — it wasn't meant to . . . get him.

HEAD. There, there Miss Millar . . . you're overcome . . . ambulance . . . exhaustion . . . nerves . . . we've all been through a great ordeal . . . (LYNNE *looks at* TON *who has the* KID *at his feet.*)

LYNNE. I didn't mean —

TON. Okay Lynne, I'll follow you down.

   LYNNE *hesitates.*

LYNNE. I didn't . . . trick you . . . believe me . . . please . . . it's important that you can . . . believe someone.

   The KID spits in her face. She cries and goes.

   Pause.

   TON *kicks the* KID. *He laughs. The* HEAD *leaves.* TON *kicks the* KID *again. The* KID *cries.* TON *kicks savagely. The* KID *whimpers.* TON *steps back.*

   Blackout.

End of play

Curtain music: Stones: 19th Nervous Breakdown.

GETAWAY

The third part of GIMME SHELTER

GETAWAY was first produced on 1 February 1977 at the Soho Poly Theatre Club, London, along with the first two plays of the *Gimme Shelter* trilogy. The cast was as follows:

KEV	Phillip Joseph
JANET	Sharman MacDonald
GARY	Ian Sharp
KID	Philip Davis

The setting is the boundary of a cricket pitch.

Music:
Before the play: hit singles from last summer
After the play: Rolling Stones' *Gimme Shelter* from the album, *Let It Bleed*.

Before lights up, music: Hit singles from last summer.
Lights up to reveal a cricket pitch boundary with the sight screen
stage right. There are two deck-chairs: KEV sits in one wearing
cricket whites and pads, reading a newspaper which covers his
face.
Enter JANET eating ice cream; she is discernibly pregnant. The
music fades.

JANET. Bloody liberty. Twenty p. a cornet and not even a bit of
flakey chocolate on the top. At least for twenty p. you'd
expect a bit of chocolate on the top. I reckon they saw me
coming.

KEV (*still behind his paper*). Need to be deaf and myopic not to
see you coming.

JANET. And the queue! Had to queue up for quarter of an
hour. If he'd have sold out — if he'd have sold out I don't
know what I'd have done. There'll be no ice cream this afternoon, and then what?

KEV (*putting down the paper*). You have posed a very intelligent
hypothesis. Spain without bullfights — there'd be a revolution.
Russia without vodka, they'd occupy the Kremlin. Deny the
Chinese rice and rickshaws, the Irish spuds and Guinness, the
Israelis circumcision and you have, potentially, a World War
Three situation. Deny the Bank Holiday cricket match with
Essex Division ice cream with flakey chocolate and — the
entire capitalist world begins to tremble . . .

JANET. I don't know what you're talking about half the time.

KEV. Gary's a selfish bastard. Fifty-six — I'll be bloody lucky to
get an innings unless he lashes out a bit.

JANET. I'm right knackered. You'd be surprised how tiring it is
walking around with this all day.

KEV. Sit down then Janet. Sit down for gawd's sake — take the
weight off your pins.

JANET. Yeah. (*She sits.*) This is putting me right off the idea of
one of them Red Indian slings.

KEV. You what?

JANET. Them Red Indian slings. You know, like the squaws

carry their kids round in on the reservations. On their back, instead of in a carrycot. It's supposed to be easier. Like you don't feel the weight so much at the back — it's easier to move. You know — like they say Hillman Imps are better 'cause the engine's at the back.

KEV. Definitely.

JANET. Mind you, I'll look nice with a little bundle on me back as I go up the High Street. I'll look like —

KEV. Parachute squad on urban manouevres.

JANET. Watch it — I might set Harry on you . . . when he gets here.

KEV. What's up with Harry boy — thought he might have been here today.

JANET. Bank Holidays are so good for fares. Especially Jewish Bank Holidays. He trebles his usual takings.

KEV. Yeah . . . blimey, you do look lovely Jan. I fancy you more than I did last year. If someone last year had told me that twelve months later you'd be married to a taxi driver with a bun in your oven —

JANET. Yeah I know . . . still don't know how it happened. When I threw up after the New Year's Eve party I must have thrown up me birth pill and all.

KEV. The thought of it put me right off potato salad. Give us a bite of that ice cream. You might have got me one.

JANET. Daren't . . . in case it put you off your stroke. Since they told you you were in the team you haven't eaten a proper lunch for . . . days.

KEV. Give us a nibble. (*He goes to her, tickles her, laughs.*)

JANET. Kev — I'm a married lady.

KEV. You still turn me on rotten Janet.

JANET. I'm different now. I'm not like that. A door has closed.

KEV. You might have let me get through it first.

Laughter. Enter the KID. *He is carrying some gardening tools. He watches.* JANET *suddenly becomes aware of him and pushes* KEV *away. Pause. The* KID *just stands there.*

JANET. You looking for someone, love? (*Pause.*) Are you

London office or Essex Division? (*Pause.*) Right chatterbox, ain't you.

KEV. You all right, son?

KID. Groundsman.

KEV. O. It's a lovely pitch. Beautiful wicket. When I saw that wicket I says to Janet here, there's love. And graft. And know-how. Best wicket I've played on all season.

JANET. The only one.

KEV. All right, all right. Mouth. (*To the* KID.) Beautiful pitch.

KID. Mr Arnold does the wicket, and the pitch. I do the drive-way and around the pavilion. The pitch — that's Mr Arnold. He's done it for forty-five years.

KEV. Beautiful, the driveway and around the pavilion and all.

KID. O.

Pause. Applause off.

KEV. What was that?

JANET. Gary — another six!

KEV. Bastard.

JANET. Fantastic!

KEV. Remember what your doctor said — don't over-excite yourself.

JANET. I'll try and keep calm when you're in.

KEV. Yeah. Not mocking. Tail-ender, apart from the openers and the middle-order, the tail-ender can make or break a team. Bondy and Leigh Hunt told me. They said that, when they asked if I was available for selection. They've put a lot of faith in me . . .

JANET. O yeah.

KEV. A lot of responsibility . . . bringing up the rear.

KID. Do you work for them?

JANET. O yeah. See, it's the firm's match. Every Bank Holiday, with Essex Division, every year . . . we always win. We're Holborn. And we always win.

KEV. Always. Curious phenomenon, in a funny way. City

Slickers. Hours on the underground . . . cramped living conditions — you'd think this country mob, fresh air, endless pastures, smell of cow-dung in their nostrils — you'd think they'd steam-roller us, but we always win. Landslide, last year.

JANET. Last year . . . (*She laughs. Teases* KEV.) Remember last year, Kev . . . over there . . .

KEV. A lot can happen in a year.

KID. I'll drink to that.

Pause.

JANET. Right revolting you was last year . . . eh Kev. Thought you was going to . . . blow 'em up! (*Pause.*) Just sulked instead. (*She touches* KEV's *hair, matily.*)

KID. Blow 'em up . . . ?

KEV. She's . . . exaggerating.

JANET. Oh yeah? Clive Jenkins? The 'revolution'? But . . . no explosion! Wouldn't be right, would it — for a trainee manager!

KEV. Double luncheon vouchers . . . I conned 'em.

The KID *laughs, surprising them.*

KID. No . . . blood and bone hanging from the ceiling . . . like Christmas decorations . . .?

JANET *and* KEV *exchange a glance.*

Funny smell burning flesh . . . hangs in the air for ages . . . (*He kneels and takes his tools out of an ex-Army kit-bag.*) It's going to be a good autumn for chrysanths . . . soil here is so rich . . . Mr Arnold says the clay below holds it in . . . the goodness . . . nothing is wasted . . .

KEV *is clearly interested in him. He watches the* KID *as he cleans the gardening tools with great care.*

JANET. Such a relief to be able to keep me Polaroids on when you're sunbathing. This pair lets the ultra-violet rays through. Do you remember that year on the beach when you was drunk and you slept all afternoon and me and Gary put your sunglasses on you and when you woke up, where you'd gone red, around your eyes you looked like Coco the Clown?

She laughs, eyes closed behind her glasses. KEV *is still studying the* KID.

KID. What you looking at?

KEV. Eh?

KID. Ain't no-one told you it's rude to stare?

KEV. What?

KID. 'No-one ever told you, boy, it's rude to stare?' Slap. Smash in the face. Didn't mean to hit him with the bike . . . bang, hit . . .slap . . . pain in me head . . . blew a fuse . . . O. (*His expression switches from defiance to humility. He looks down and cleans his tools again.*)

KEV *puts a cigarette in his own mouth and offers the packet to the* KID.

KEV. Do you smoke?

The KID *grins.*

KID. No. Not now. Don't smoke. Used to. Not now.

KEV. Better for your health.

KID. Better for everyone else's health.

'Howzat?' off.

KEV. Hello, hello!

JANET. Kev — Gary's had it!

KEV. Out!

JANET. Just Winston and you're in!

KEV. O, I can't wait to get out there. The way that bloody mob of provincials are bowling — Christ, it'll be like playing ping-pong with a tennis racket. I hope that sodding house magazine photographer hasn't used up all his film. I'll give him a few spectacular shots. (*He's miming them.*) Sort of balletic, all-action snaps that'll have the Tate Gallery begging him to make an exhibition.

Enter GARY.

Unlucky son, unlucky. Know what you did wrong?

GARY. Swung too hard.

KEV. You swung too hard.

GARY. Still, sixty-two ain't bad.

KEV. O, it isn't bad. I'll grant you that. In fact, a lot of people d

say it was very good. I mean, Bondy, put it this way, Bondy
would have been bloody delighted to have got sixty-two. The
only thing is . . .

GARY. What?

KEV. Well, it was all — look, you don't mind me giving you an
analytical breakdown of where you went wrong, do you?

GARY. Well —

KEV. Frankly, your innings — well, it was distinctly lacking in,
how shall I put it? Artistry . . .

GARY. Bullshit.

KEV. Hardly a contribution to the literature of the game. Not a
phrase synonymous with John Arlott or to be found idly
flicking through the pages of Wisden's — not a word that leaps
out at you.

GARY. Artistry, my arse. Sixty-two —

KEV. Good innings, good innings. What I'm saying is — it was all
a bit hurried. A bit rushed. No stylised defensive shots, not
much off the ol' back foot. No sussing the field and planting
nonchalant lobs tantalisingly behind the outlying fielders, you
know. The sort of shots that dip just behind cover point and
then the bastard has to turn round and give chase to save a
four. In vain.

GARY. Kev, I lashed out and got seven sixes.

KEV. That might impress some people —

GARY. Well, blimey. Seven sixes are better than fucking
tantalising lobs for four.

KEV. You watch me. I'll show you what I mean. Take me time,
a bit of artistry. O, what a cool arrogant bastard, they'll say.
He's taking his time.

GARY. We need thirty-five from ten overs — got to hurry.

KEV. Ah son, you are confusing speed for hurry. It's like making
love and fucking — there's a difference.

JANET. O yeah?

KEV. Anyone can fuck. Not many make love. Making love is
like serenading on a rare violin. Elephants fuck, you don't
get —

JANET. Elephants playing the violin.

GARY. Right! (*He laughs.*) You are a bloody joker, Kev.

KEV. All right, as you like it. They'll be pleased with you tonight Gary. Oh yeah, tonight at the dance, they'll be pretty pleased with you. Of course, the geezer that'll find himself the focus of all the attention'll be the geezer who rattles up the winning run but —

Roars off.

Fuck.

GARY. Winston . . . six.

KEV. Must be bloody contagious. (*He shouts.*) Take it easy boy. Take it easy. (*He sighs.*) There'll be some champagne bubbling tonight, boy. Some corks exploding.

JANET. There's thirty crates. I saw them. Bondy's receptionist told me Bondy had selected them personally himself. He phoned up this chateau in France and got them to fly it all over specially. Bondy has got style —

KEV. I'm surprised Bondy ain't started walking on the fucking water yet.

GARY. He knows about champagne. That do at the Savoy, the wine waiter said Bondy knew more than he did.

KEV. What do at the Savoy?

GARY. For the . . . when the Germans came over.

KEV. You went, did you?

GARY. Yeah.

KEV. I see.

GARY. Six of us from the trainee management course —

KEV. I remember. I was pretty tied up with the Birmingham office then. Sorting out their accounts. Champagne we got through that night. I was cleaning me teeth with it. (*He suddenly becomes again aware of the* KID.) I bet all this sounds terribly bourgeois to you, eh?

Pause.

I know what you're thinking. I thought it at one time. But don't let apparent appearances deceive you. Oh how fucking bourgeois, I expect you're saying to yourself. Am I right, is that what you're saying?

KID. I dunno what it means . . .

KEV. Ah — you need a political education son.

GARY. From who? (*He laughs.*) Got a beer there Jan — I'm gasping.

JANET. Bit warm, but I kept it covered up with me jumper.

GARY *looks at her.*

GARY. Always keep your jumper on to keep it warm . . . .

Pause.

JANET. Yeah well . . . don't have to pay for taxis.

GARY. Right.

JANET. What did she say?

GARY. Eh?

JANET. Clare?

GARY. O —

KEV. Clare!

JANET. I'm surprised Bondy brought her, with his wife here.

KEV. What you going on about?

JANET. Well, it's obvious.

KEV. Obvious?

JANET. I mean, if his wife sees just, well, just the way Clare looks at Bondy . . . then she'll know.

KEV. Know? Know what?

JANET. Don't be naive.

KEV. You what?

JANET. Everybody knows.

KEV. If everybody knows, how come I ain't got the foggiest idea what you're going on about.

JANET. Him and her — Clare.

KEV. Bondy and Clare —

JANET. Perhaps they only discuss it at the directors' Christmas parties.

KEV. O, that explains it! That's how you speak with such pontifical authority — if it's only discussed at the directors' Christmas parties.

JANET. You know how they used to invite me. Like how now they invite the young girls in typing and that . . . Funny, there being younger girls now. Me talking to the older women, about relaxation classes and that. What did Clare say to you then?

GARY. Well, nothing — she just looked.

JANET. Took long enough.

KEV. Wonder she can bloody see at all with all that crap round her eyes. Looks like she's been peering through a pair of binoculars with the lenses smothered in black emulsion paint.

JANET. What if she makes a pass at you at the dance tonight?

GARY. Leave off!

JANET. Just to get at Bondy — for bringing his wife.

KEV. Eh?

JANET. O, don't be so naive, Kev. Everyone knows how he takes Clare on all his trips . . . Munich and Amsterdam and Paris and the conferences at Blackpool.

KEV. How very cosmopolitan. There is nothing more disgusting than bourgeois gossip —

KID. What?

Pause.

KEV. Bourgeois . . . (*Pause.*) French. (*Pause.*) Middle class. Wider connotations, in a political focus as it were . . . synonymous with — *the enemy.*

Longer pause.

KID. Whose enemy?

KEV. Exactly!

JANET. Winston's arf put on weight.

GARY. Eh?

JANET. Last year he looked so slim . . . and now look at him.

KEV. All them bloody accountants' lunches. To be an accountant, you need a strong stomach more than a head for figures.

GARY. You want a beer, mate?

KID. O . . . I can't take it.

GARY. Course you can.

KID. For me?

GARY. Yeah.

KID. Mr Arnold drinks half a bottle of whisky a day. Sometimes the boundary line has a bend in it. He says he's looping the loop. (*He laughs. The others don't.*)

(*Pause.*) All right, tar. (*He opens the can. Cuts his finger.*) Shit! Bloody tin.

JANET. It's bleeding —

GARY. Blimey, you bleed easily.

JANET. Let it bleed, that's the best thing. Clears out any germs . . . just let it bleed.

The KID *holds up a dripping, bloody finger and stares at it with fascination.*

Put it away, do me a favour — it's making me stomach turn.

KID. There was a bloke . . .

Pause.

In Feltham . . . he got a razor blade . . . they took them away but he saved them up . . . he took the mattress off his bed, and where there was the wooden frame, he made slits, and stuck the razor blades in them . . . they all stood up . . . some was broken. He ran into the door, with his head . . . metal door, like cells are . . . and when he was really dizzy, he threw himself on the bed and the blades went in here and here and here and here . . . and one went in his throat. I emptied his shit bucket and filled it with water and washed up the blood . . . and I never saw him again.

Silence.

JANET. I'm going to get some ice creams, would anyone like one?

They ignore her and she goes.

GARY. Feltham?

KID. Nine months.

GARY. What is it?

KID. Ain't Butlins.

KEV. It's a kinda Borstal . . . in't it?

KID. For loons. (*He giggles, pause.*) I ain't a loon.

GARY. What did you do?

KID. Nothin'.

GARY. Then why —

KID. What I nearly did.

GARY. What?

KID. B . . . b . . . blow 'em up!

GARY. Who?

KID. Me school . Last day . . . they was shitting themselves. Got this . . . pain in me head. I didn't know what I was doing. Didn't mean it. At Feltham, this trick cyclist . . . he said at least it would have been better if I'd meant it. He said then he'd have understood.

KEV. You tried to . . . blow up your school?

KID. Leave off, not the whole school. I ain't no Guy Fawkes. Just some of the people in it . . . with me motorbike . . . didn't do it . . .

Pause.

KEV. In Rainham.

KID. Yeah.

KEV. I read about it. In the papers. It was you. It was you!

KID. They didn't say who it was. They weren't allowed to use me name — 'cause I'm a juvenile.

KEV. All that, and they don't even use your name. Anonymous. That's a bastard.

KID. Nar.

KEV. O Christ, O Christ! Don't you remember, Gary? Christ, the publicity! Papers full of it. Afterwards, Panorama did a whole programme — 'The Twilight World of Educational No-Hopers.' Robin Day got his glasses steamed up with Roy Hattersley and —

KID. I must've missed that.

KEV. Even Maggie Thatcher got in on the act. Said this was exactly what you expected when inflation ran at 16 per cent.

KID. I didn't know what none of them was on about.

KEV. And no-one said it was you. No name. Never.

KID. Glad about that. Me mum had to go on tranquillisers and her hair went white. (*Pause.*) Here, I'm not allowed to talk about it. When Mr Arnold took me on it was on the strict understanding that no-one knew about it. If anyone knows, I'll be out on me arse.

KEV. You can rely on me.

KID. Hard getting a job after Borstal. This place here, they're very good. They take you on. I'm going.

   KID *attempts to go.* KEV *holds him.*

KEV. Hang about, hang about. I want to shake you by the hand.

KID. What?

KEV. I want to shake you by the hand.

KID. Eh?

KEV. Your hand.

KID. It's still bleeding.

KEV. Scars of the revolution. Like me.

KID. Eh?

KEV. Daren't take me shirt off when I'm sunbathing. Less the scars of the class struggle on me back show. Frighten the horses.

GARY. Clare's finger-nails.

KEV. Sit down son, sit down. (*He forces the* KID *into a chair.*)

KID. Nar, gotta go, gotta getaway.

KEV. An' old colonels, kept writing letters to *The Times.* 'Is this what is meant by Socialist comprehensive education?' Like it was all part of the liberal studies curriculum, or something.

KID. Look, I don't wanna talk about it. It's over. Something that happened. I've served me time, repaid me debt to society and all that, right. I've started again. School, waste of bleeding time. Feltham though, showed me how to . . . give me a trade. Fantastic job. Out all weathers. All summer, out in the open. I was in charge of the vegetable gardens. Growed things, and ate 'em. Learned a lot. Got it made now. When I left, the governor, he said to me: 'You've achieved two things. Learned a trade. Gardener. And you've found respect in yourself.' (*Slight pause.*) I've got respect in meself now.

KEV. For Christ's sake. You had more respect in your little toenail the day you —

KID (*leaps out of the chair*). Shut up! Don't talk about it!

KEV. For Christ's sake, why not?

KID. 'Cause I wanna forget about it, right! In the past, don't wanna keep looking back. Mistake. Made a mistake. Now, forget it, look forward to stuff. Got respect, ain't I? Make a go of things. Not keep raking up last year.

KEV (*forcing the* KID *back into the chair. Impassioned*). That's what I'm saying. That's why I want to shake your hand, son. 'Cause it was . . . a start. It . . . thrilled me.

KID. I dunno what you're talking about.

KEV. For Christ's sake! Can't you see it? It thrilled hundreds, it thrilled thousands, what you did. It gave hope. Your great gesture, a spark of the inevitable . . . revolution. It should be blazed across England.

GARY. Leave him alone, Kev.

KID. He don't understand.

KEV. But I *do* understand. I do. You did, you did what I wanted to do. You did it.

KID. Bollocks.

KEV (*holding the* KID *in the chair, almost pleading*). I'm serious. Felt your anger. Your rage. You took the great leap and let it go.

KID. I didn't let it go, thank Christ I didn't let it go.

KEV. I wish you had done.

KID. You're mad. (*To* GARY.) He's mad, in't he?

KEV. Wish, it had gone further. The supreme gesture.

KID. Look, I'm all straight now, so don't you start messing me up.

KEV. I'm not messing you up. It's them, over there, them up
there, them who dash up and down compromising, keeping
the status quo in balance, they're the ones who're the ones
who're messing you up. What you did . . . you was right.

KID. Stop trying to . . . mix me up. I've got it together now.

KEV. You gave hope. You breathed life into the dream that . . .
things, this England . . . 1976 . . . can be changed.

KID. I've changed.

KEV. For the worse.

KID. Don't you fucking tell me. I'm not getting mixed up again.
I'm happy now.

KEV. What, watering the dahlias?

KID. You're mad.

KEV. What if when Lenin got the call in Zurich, what if he'd
said — 'Sorry mate, I've got to weed me window box'?

KID. I dunno what you're talking about.

KEV. Jesus, kid — what I'm saying is, thank you, for that
inspiration. We all know everything's wrong. But there's gotta
be a moment when it can all . . . happen. Your moment,
showed it ain't a dream.

KID. A dream? I fucking dreamed about it, in Feltham. Fucking
nightmare. That I dropped the fag, the petrol went and the
bodies burned. The eyes popped. The bellies exploded. Burned
flesh, like sticky black plastic, stuck to me face, closed me
eyes, I couldn't see.

KEV. Yeah, well — what I'm saying is: Your anger, your rage . . .
I know that rage. Could have been me in that room. Got to
unify angers. Not waste it. Together we —

KID. We?

Silence

Shake me by the hand, you say. Might get yours dirty.

KEV. We're on the same side. We are. Look on me as . . . like the
Red Cross. Behind the lines. Patching up the warriors. Sending
them back over the top. Fifth column. Infiltrating. Ready to
use the knowledge I've absorbed —

GARY. Kev!

KEV. What?

GARY. Kev, you've changed sides.

KEV. Haven't, haven't! Just . . . look like it. See you kid, I see myself. See I was right.

Pause.

KID (*stands up, derisive*). I'll leave it to you then. (*He picks up the tools.*) You make me laugh. (*He begins to go, turns, laughs.*) Ain't had such a good laugh for ages.

The KID *has gone. Pause.* KEV *shouts after him.*

KEV. You can't walk away from your rage. You can't walk away from it. Day'll come they'll chant your name. Whatever it is.

GARY. Winston, only need two to win.

KEV. Dunno what . . . just know I gotta . . . (*He sits wearily.*) I might as well take off the pads . . .

Pause.

GARY. You never know, way he's slogging, you could go in . . . Only need two to win.

KEV. I'll take off the pads. (*He begins to take off the pads.*)

GARY. Moving in the fielders . . . tricky end and all . . . from the sea-front . . . rubbing the ball.

Enter JANET.

JANET. You'll never guess — Pia's here and guess what, she's going to have twins!

GARY. Hang on Janet . . . look —

JANET. What?

GARY. Winston . . . only need two runs to win.

JANET. Oh yea . . . Pia's having twins, did you hear Kev? Pia, she's so happy . . . and the mortgage has come through, this lovely place at Hornchurch, a bit too expensive, she said, but they've got the mortgage over thirty years so they can afford it . . . and they'll all be moved in, out of that rotten flat and have the house decorated and ready in time for the birth, oh how smashing. See, I told her not to give up hope, when they was living with his in-laws, and however terrible it seemed then, I knew it'd work out for the best.

GARY. And here it comes . . .

The light begins to fade. KEV sits, head in hands, slumped in his deckchair. JANET and GARY both look at the pitch expectantly. Applause.

We've won. (*He looks at KEV.*) Again . . .

A very slow fade. Fade in Rolling Stones' Gimme Shelter. *The three characters freeze as light fades slowly to blackout and volume of music increases.*

End of play.

OTHER GROVE PRESS DRAMA AND THEATER PAPERBACKS

B415   ARDEN, JOHN / Plays: One (Serjeant Musgrave's Dance, The
Workhouse Donkey, Armstrong's Last Goodnight) / $4.95

E611   ARRABAL, FERNANDO / Garden of Delights / $2.95

E96   BECKETT, SAMUEL / Endgame / $1.95

E318   BECKETT, SAMUEL / Happy Days / $2.45

E33   BECKETT, SAMUEL / Waiting for Godot / $1.95 [See also
Seven Plays of the Modern Theater, Harold Clurman, ed. E717 /
$6.95]

B79   BEHAN, BRENDAN / The Quare Fellow* and The Hostage: Two
Plays / $2.95 *[See also Seven Plays of the Modern Theater,
Harold Clurman, ed. E717 / $6.95]

B120   BRECHT, BERTOLT / Galileo / $1.95

B414   BRECHT, BERTOLT / The Mother / $2.95

B333   BRECHT, BERTOLT / The Threepenny Opera / $1.95

E717   CLURMAN, HAROLD / Seven Plays of the Modern Theater
(Waiting for Godot by Samuel Beckett, The Quare Fellow by
Brendan Behan, A Taste of Honey by Shelagh Delaney, The
Connection by Jack Gelber, The Balcony by Jean Genet,
Rhinoceros by Eugene Ionesco, The Birthday Party by Harold
Pinter) / $6.95]

E344   DURRENMATT, FRIEDRICH / The Visit / $2.95

E130   GENET, JEAN / The Balcony / $2.95

E208   GENET, JEAN / The Blacks: A Clown Show / $2.95

E577   GENET, JEAN / The Maids and Deathwatch: Two Plays / $3.95

E456   IONESCO, EUGENE / Exit the King / $2.95

E101   IONESCO, EUGENE / Four Plays (The Bald Soprano, The
Lesson, The Chairs, Jack or The Submission) / $2.95

E679   IONESCO, EUGENE / Man With Bags / $3.95

E259   IONESCO, EUGENE / Rhinoceros and Other Plays (The
Leader, The Future is in Eggs, or It Takes All Sorts to Make a
World) / $2.45

E496   JARRY, ALFRED / The Ubu Plays (Ubu Rex, Ubu Cuckolded,
Ubu Enchained) / $3.95

E697   MAMET, DAVID / American Buffalo / $3.95

E709   MAMET, DAVID / A Life in the Theatre / $3.95

E712   MAMET, DAVID / Sexual Perversity in Chicago and The Duck
Variations / $3.95

E716   MAMET, DAVID / The Water Engine and Mr. Happiness: Two
Plays / $3.95

B400   ORTON, JOE / The Complete Plays (The Ruffian on the Stair,
The Good and Faithful Servant, The Erpingham Camp, Funeral
Games, Loot, What the Butler Saw, Entertaining Mr. Sloane) /
$4.95

B402 PINTER, HAROLD / Complete Works: One (The Birthday Party, The Room, The Dumb Waiter, A Slight Ache, A Night Out, The Black and White, The Examination) / $3.95

B403 PINTER, HAROLD / Complete Works: Two (The Caretaker, Night School, The Dwarfs, The Collection, The Lover, Five Revue Sketches) / $3.95

B410 PINTER, HAROLD / Complete Works: Three (Landscape, Silence, The Basement, Six Revue Sketches, Tea Party [play], Tea Party [short story], Mac) / $3.95

E411 PINTER, HAROLD / The Homecoming / $1.95

E555 PINTER, HAROLD / Landscape and Silence: Two Plays / $3.95

E663 PINTER, HAROLD / No Man's Land / $1.95

E635 SHEPARD, SAM / The Tooth of Crime and Geography of a Horse Dreamer: Two Plays / $3.95

E684 STOPPARD, TOM / Dirty Linen and New-Found-Land: Two Plays / $2.95

E703 STOPPARD, TOM / Every Good Boy Deserves Favor and Professional Foul: Two Plays / $3.95

B319 STOPPARD, TOM / Rosencrantz and Guildenstern Are Dead / $1.95

E434 VIAN, BORIS / The Generals' Tea Party / $1.95

E62 WALEY, ARTHUR, tr. and ed. / The No Plays of Japan / $5.95

E519 WOOD, CHARLES / Dingo / $1.95

CRITICAL STUDIES

E127 ARTAUD, ANTONIN / The Theater and Its Double / $3.95

E441 COHN, RUBY, ed. / Casebook on Waiting for Godot / $3.95

E603 HARRISON, PAUL CARTER / The Drama of Nommo: Black Theater in the African Continuum / $2.45

E695 HAYMAN, RONALD / How To Read A Play / $2.95

E387 IONESCO, EUGENE / Notes and Counternotes: Writings on the Theater / $3.95

GROVE PRESS, INC., 196 West Houston St., New York, N.Y. 10014